A Timeless Teaching

dovidHouse
publishing

Copyright © 2021 by dovid Krafchow

All rights reserved. No part of this book may be reproduced or used in any manner without written permission of the copyright owner except for the use of quotations in a book review.

ISBN: 978-1-7376567-2-2

www.dovidhouse.com

ZOHAR

Beneath The Black Whole

dovid Krafchow

TABLE OF CONTENTS

Timeline	06
Foreword	09
Introduction	13
Preface	15
Part One: The Past	**21**
Chapter One	*page 21*
Chapter Two	*page 27*
Chapter Three	*page 33*
Chapter Four	*page 41*
Chapter Five	*page 47*
Chapter Six	*page 51*
Chapter Seven	*page 57*
Chapter Eight	*page 65*
Chapter Nine	*page 71*
Chapter Ten	*page 77*
Part Two: The Present	**85**
Chapter One	*page 85*
Chapter Two	*page 91*
Chapter Three	*page 97*
Chapter Four	*page 103*
Chapter Five	*page 109*
Chapter Six	*page 117*
Chapter Seven	*page 123*
Chapter Eight	*page 129*
Chapter Nine	*page 135*
Chapter Ten	*page 141*
The Future	147
Conclusion	161
Afterword	169
Fornication Under Consent of the King	171

Time line

0 —	266,450,000 years that God played with creation before the creating of the human being.
1 —	Sixth Day of Creation; beginning of Hebrew calendar.
666 —	Chanoch; beginning of Mayan calendar.
1666 —	Noah's Flood.
1998 —	Tower of Babel.
2000 —	Avraham leaves Tower of Babel.
2025 —	Avraham comes to the Earth.
2087 —	Ishmael born; Arabic.
2100 —	Yitzchok born; Hebrew.
2448 —	Moshe establishes Jewish People by leaving Egypt.
2928 —	First Temple erected.
3338 —	First Temple destroyed after 410 years.
3410 —	Second Temple erected after 70 years in exile.
3761 —	Roman Empire begins.
3830 (70) —	Second Temple destroyed after 420 year.
3979 (149) —	Oral Torah is written down called, Mishna.

4186 (206) —	Talmud compiled.
4330 (570) —	Mohammed born; Koran; Mayan calendar.
4800 (1040) —	Rashi commentary on Torah.
5240 (1480) —	Inquisition in Spain; Americas discovered.
5666 (1906) —	E=MC2, San Francisco earthquake, cubism.
5680 (1920) —	World War One; Europe divides up Middle East.
5700 (1940) —	World War Two.
5704 (1944) —	Atomic bomb.
5708 (1948) —	Israeli State.
5730 (1970) —	Half-life of Carbon-14.
5740 (1980) —	Gog and Magog; Reagan and Pope installed.
5758 (1998) —	Earth hit by neutron star for five minutes.
2759 (1999) —	Hebrew calendar spells out Satan/Opposer.
5760 (2000) —	Roman calendar ends, Bush last Roman Emperor.
5763 (2003) —	Planet Mars comes closest to Earth; Roman war.
5765 (2005) —	Hurricane Katrina precipitates end of Rome.
5772 (2012) —	End of Mayan calendar after 5,106 years.
5777 (2017) —	Eclipse across Bible Belt; Trump elected.
5780 (2080) —	Paradigm Shift; Thousand Years of Woman.

Foreword

The Harlequin Divide
Time and Space
Elucidated

The number 666 has been predominate in my life from the very beginning. My social security number begins 5666 which in the Hebrew calendar was 1906 when Einstein published his famous equation E=MC2 a week before Rosh HaShana/New Year 5666. When my publicist asked me how to describe myself; after some reflection, I suggested: Einstein on Acid. Besides the number 666, there are other associations I share with the famous Jewish physicists. Einstein published two books within one year which changed the course of the world by revealing a new paradigm, quantum physics. Between September 29, 2020 and August 17, 2021 I released my two book treatise: The Harlequin Divide—Time and Space Elucidated taking quantum physics to a new level.

There is another association with the number 666 serving as my basis for fifty years of study culminating with these two books: **Zohar— Beyond and Beneath the BlackWhole**. A week after Rosh HaShana/ New Year 5666 a Rebbe in Russia began a weekly publication spanning three years and was later compiled into a book called: **666**. Einstein explained how light pulsates between ray and matter while at the same time, the Rebbe explained how time is incorporated into light and what precedes time. These two Jewish intellects converge around the number 666, Einstein a week before and the Rebbe one week after Rosh HaShana/New Year 5666. After clarifying the source of light in the beginning of the book **666**, the Rebbe goes on to describe how to get to the source of light.

Using the metaphor of water, the Rebbe explains the difference between Collected Waters and Living Waters. The Torah, the Teaching of the Jewish People, defines Living Waters as seven years of continual flow. Accordingly, there are two types of scholars, one considered the Lips of Truth and the other Truth. Lesser scholars speak in general terms, far from the Truth and even further than the Source. The scholars with great minds and sharp intellects are unable to get to the Source because they are blinded by their own light and the clarity of their understanding. The Rebbe goes on to explain the third and deepest level called the Truth of Truth is the Source. Only the inept ones blessed with inspiration are motivated to dig deep and overcoming obstacles eventually warranting the Source of the Truth.

The Rebbe demonstrates the advantage of digging deep and overcoming obstacles as seen in the unique way information coming from the Source transmitted through the conduit of the inept is conveyed. Enduring this long and arduous process renders a revelation like none other. Understanding life comes from accruing knowledge; knowing happens through experience—the knowledge of life. I have spent fifty years digging through the hard ground of paved over reality before divulging this knowledge in a book called: **Sex a Metaphor to History—Trump 777 and the Thousand Years of Woman** published on September 29, 2020 under the pen name, dovid B. Timeless. What prompted this book was the culmination of Trumpism. There was common knowledge, if Trump was elected for a second term, America would be destroyed. I wanted to lend a hand in his defeat.

I felt an intense interest pushing me from Heaven. When I finished the book in late August, I felt compelled to publish the book before the election to illuminate the meaning behind the three occurrences of the number 777. The year the eclipse crossed the Bible Belt of America in 2017/5777 was also the year Trump was elected, a clear sign from Heaven. The day Trump was inaugurated he was seventy years, seven months and seven days, corroborating the sign from Heaven. Later, on March 11, 2020 when Covid was declared a pandemic, there were exactly 7,770,000 people in the world—God was yelling at the world to stop. In Hebrew, the word Covid means Respect. Those in charge had lost respect for the world and the people populating the Earth, all of whom God loves.

Being a person of numbers, I immediately understood what was being said and hurried to write and publish my modest book hoping this spiritual information made available to the world would make a difference in the outcome the election. The day after I published my book, Trump announce he and his family had come down with Covid. The world had come to a juncture in time. I took the opportunity in my book to explain the genesis of time, the scope of time and most importantly, the symmetry of time. I hurried to published my book. I had neither the money or time to employ an editor, so I went over the book again and again before publishing **Sex a Metaphor to History—Trump 777 and the Thousand Years of Woman**. Nonetheless, my beautiful little book is flawed by occasional typos. I ask the reader's forbearance, It seems to me, since this is truly new information, I should retain the original manuscript, preserving the initial flawed iteration.

The limited publication of **Sex a Metaphor to History—Trump 777 and the Thousand Years of Woman** prompted another book explaining space, called: **Zohar—Beyond the BlackWhole** which was published August 17, 2021. The harlequin nature of time and space plus the abject different rendering of each subject along with copyright restraints caused the final rendition of **Sex a Metaphor to History—Trump 777 and the Thousand Years of Woman** into a new edition. **Zohar—Beneath the BlackWhole** explains the essence of time. **Zohar—Beyond the BlackWhole** explains the essence of space. Together they represent the harlequin divide of time and space elucidated.

Lastly, the profanity-laced text in Zohar—Beneath the BlackWhole compared with the celestial language in Zohar—Beyond the BlackWhole requires an explanation, I offer this precedent from the words of a teacher in Russia, an adherent to the Rebbe wrote the book 5666. The teacher taught at the risk of his life a small cadre of students who cajoled a prominent rabbi to come and hear their teacher teach.

The rabbi took up the offer. The students brought the rabbi to their underground meeting place. The rabbi came in with his aplomb, straightened his long silken black coat, set his perfectly manicured hat on his head then sat down to hear the words of the teacher. The teacher eyed the man for a moment and then said, "You look to me like one of those hairs between the asshole and the balls."

The rabbi was stunned. He stood up, adjusted his long black coat, set his black hat upon his head and left. After a long silence one of the students dared to ask their beloved teacher, "Why did you say that?"

The teacher looked up and replied, "That's all he could understand."

Introduction

Time viewed as a line can only be broken up into eras, but time plotted in a spiral reveals the form of creation. Sex, more than any other human attribute is intrinsically tied to time. Sex has a time, suddenly spontaneously aroused when clarity arises. Pregnancy has an exact nine month time schedule. The sex act has a beginning when man enters in, then there is a middle time while man plows the soil before finally planting the seed. Many human endeavors are liken to sex, where a commitment incurred through love, brings about work focused at a goal to be redeemed sometime in the future as Pleasure.

A spiral is more sexy than a line or even a circle because a spiral is made from the line of the man integrated into the circle of woman, coming together for a common purpose: to reach climax together. Why should human history be any different? History appears careening in an ever-changing tide merging with the infinite ocean of time, but what if time were segmented into a beginning, middle and end? The five thousand year Mayan calendar and the six thousand year Hebrew calendar begin and end at a precise moment.

The six thousand year calendar begins with the creation of man into a feminine world where woman is hidden. The five thousand year Mayan calendar begins 666 years later, as if the 666 is conception slated to conclude five thousand years in the future. The ancients saw into the future and termed our time, the End of Days when the calendars end. Six, the line of man, enters into the circle of seven as the world begins the long awaited, Thousand Years of Woman and Peace. Each thousand year segment cycles around the climax, towards revolution when man holds woman above himself.

Without recognizing the form of creation segmented into thousand year cycles, the power structure is able to hide behind walls of misinformation, like the Big Bang Theory, because only confusion can quell the curiosity for Truth. Religion plays a big part in hiding and skewing the Truth. Knowing where we are in time allows the freedom to express in spacial confines. Doing the right thing at the wrong time is inevitably doomed to failure, as is doing the wrong thing at the right time. Only through understanding the sequencing of time can we find our true place in creation.

The purpose of this book is to introduce the world to the concept of the coming Thousand Years of Woman and Peace happening here on Earth in the near beautiful future. Unfortunately, those traditions carrying this knowledge for thousands of years, have been unwilling to share this knowledge with the world. Though warned by the esoteric literature, not to reveal these secrets, an added caveat gives permission by saying, When the world is falling apart, teach it all. As an independent Jewish Truth seeker, I intend to reveal everything.

Preface

I began my journey into the secret of life just as I entered my 26th year; I recently turned 76, having pursued these secrets embedded in my Jewish Soul for fifty years—this book is a culmination of that journey. I joined the Navy at 17, was on the ship that started the Vietnam War, was released 1965 in San Francisco when LSD was still legal. For the next five years I hitch-hiked 30,000 miles. I was seeking a diversity of people and experiences to better understand life, so I took to the road. In many ways the Sixties was a virgin generation, since there had never been anything quite like the Sixties. Many people recognized a seed was being sown for the future and gave their lives believing in destiny; fifty years later the seed has sprouted and grown into a new perception of reality— now offering up her fruit, a pipe dream ripe to be grasped. As the Sixties ended, I abandoned the road and began studying the Torah with a hidden collection of secret seekers tracing back nine generations who had recently been transported from Russia to Brooklyn, New York. I am the tenth and final extension of that branch.

Actually, the Russians were not allowed to learn the secret. They could only learn about the secret. They were constrained from the very beginning of their dynasty nine generations earlier not to study the Zohar, but their leader in each generation would teach them what was relevant. The Rebbes in each generation wrote voluminously and by the time I arrived on the scene, hundreds of years later, the plethora of books were bubbling up into printed words like a spring destined to build into a raging river. Many books had been rumored but only a few manuscripts had been released, much had been lost during the two world wars. I was born in 1944 between D-Day June 6, 1944 and the dropping of the atomic bomb August 6, 1945. From my infancy, I recall the crematorium before being exploded back into this world.

My way to the secret has been circuitous at best, more like a drop of water slowly passing through the hard dark ground on the way to the sea. After a year with the Russians, having learned to read Hebrew and a rudimentary understanding of concepts, I left to drive a truck in New York City. After five years I left to run a one-man printshop outside of Ann Arbor, Michigan. Five years later, I moved to Israel where I lived in the ancient city of Sfat, one the four holy cities corresponding to the four elements: fire, air, water and earth. Sfat is the element of air. Across the valley from Sfat is where the Zohar was written two thousand years ago; more than a millennium later, a small gathering of hidden secret seekers caused the Ari, living in Egypt, to have a vision. The Ari followed his vision to Sfat and taught there for three years before passing away in his thirties. The Ari never wrote anything, but what he taught became the foundational light called the Cabala/Receiving. A few generations later, began the ten generations of the Chasidim. Cabala is meant for the scholar while Chasidut is meant for the people.

I have two abilities with which I have opened the secret door and discovered the Truth. My first ability is, ever since getting out of the navy and probably even before that, I don't like people telling me what to do and don't want to be owned. The other is, I am autistic. My consternation with the rabbis has only grown with time, which has been an advantage, so as not be constrained by their well tested dictates, restrictions and patterned thinking. The Talmud teaches concerning the text in the Torah: You work and you will be satiated with physical blessings. The Rabbis taught, do your physical work and God will bless you. Rabbi Shimmon, author of the Zohar taught, The study of Torah is our work, study the Torah and God will give you what you need. The Talmud concludes, Some did as Rabbis and they were successful; others did like Rabbi Shimmon and failed. Was the great Rabbi Shimmon wrong? My Russian teacher, Rav Aba, who taught me to read explained, The people who went according to Rabbi Shimmon did not know how to wait. I have taken the path of Rabbi Shimmon and I have failed throughout my life but I have waited. I have continually studied until I am ready to succeed because I have found the Truth inside the secret.

My most obvious autistic trait is my inability to remember articulated sound. As a result of this disability, particularly having to learn my first language other than English, I resorted to vision. Where others could rattle off the Hebrew prayers without a book, after fifty years, I am unable to say a line of Hebrew text without looking into a book. Even then, I often mispronounce the word, yet this also, has had unexpected rewards because no scholar would take me seriously, increasing my chances of actually finding the Truth I sought. Seeking Truth is a lonely occupation with no real reward since Truth is worth little in our false world, and as soon as you sell it, Truth loses all credibility. I remember standing on the bow of a mighty ship sliding up and down on mammoth sultry succulent ebony waves reducing the ship into a boat, thinking if I don't know what is true then how can I know what to do. This random thought, resulting from weeks of musing while crossing the biggest ocean in the world, has patterned my life. Eventually, I concluded that I was wrong, better to live your life, but I was already hooked on the journey. I wanted to know the Truth.

The point in life is to intend good, being right is just an accident. As a result, even though my actions were often errant, my intentions were pure, so God has watched over me. Thank You. My time has finally come and I am ready for the fight. Men are made to fight and being alone is how a male becomes a man. My first 25 years of life had beaten me down until I was no more than dust but from there emerged a new person who had found a path in life. I have a sharp intellect and a good memory so I went to fight with the Torah. I was equipped with pointed questions and set traps, my tongue sharp as a sword, the fallow soil of my brain was suddenly drenched in life affirming dew. My first exposure to this new path had been standing in a cramped room filled with old tombs of big thick tattered books replete with yellow pages where each letter was pressed into the paper making a permanent impression beyond the fading ink. The books were in an unfamiliar alphabet, but when I saw someone kiss a book before returning the volume to the shelf, I fell in love and wanted to learn them all.

Because I could not connect to the audio aspect of Hebrew, I read slowly, focusing on my ability to understand the vision within the word. Where others, even brilliant people who had been studying all their lives, understood transmission of concepts, I was able to comprehend the vision hiding within these archaic symbols, beyond the concept. No one could understand how I could read these books without being able to pronounce the words. Even more, they could not corroborate or refute my own unique sagacity. After a year, having acquired the rudimentary skills to unlock the Torah, I left and went on my own journey both physically through my endless meanderings on this planet and spiritually through my daily devotion to my studies. One book led to another, clarifying this specialized language fit only for honest seekers of the Truth. I became my own authority, constantly testing my vision against new information. The vast majority of the Cabala focuses on information pertaining to the attenuating spiritual light eventually seeping into our crude world. I had composed a picture in my mind of the spiritual realm funneling light into our physical reality.

I began to see how everything traces back to the Tree of Life composed on three different metaphoric levels reflected in the symmetry of trees with roots, trunk and branches replicated in the three segments of the human form: head, torso, hips. Everything began conforming to this configuration, causing physical life to take on an added spiritual dimension. I began incorporating science into my picture of creation and found many correlations; next, world history came into focus having traced back text to the genesis of language from the Tower of Babel—clarity was rushing at me and I did not duck. After thirty years of study, I decided to write down my portrait of creation, I called this first attempt, 26645 A New Cosmology and World History based on the Cabala. I sent the manuscript to the Library of Congress to validate the timing of my words since, in this book written in 1998, I predicted, based on my studies into the Tree of Life, that there would undoubtably be discovered in the near future, five moons around Pluto, the furthest planet out in our solar system made from the Sun and nine planets. Ten years later, astronomers made the same discovery and recently flew by for corroboration. I also predicted they will find oceans beneath the surface of Mars.

Since then, I left the Cabala key to the Zohar and took up learning the actual Zohar, the final and ultimate hidden text. For twenty years I have been studying the Zohar, trying to answer the fundamental claim written towards the end of the Zohar, These words are meant for the End of Days, when the calendar runs out of years. And here we are only 220 years from that end. The Zohar is written in a conglomeration of ancient Hebrew and Aramaic; with no clear direction to the free thinking storytelling in the seemingly chaotic text—yet, the Zohar answers all questions. Little by little, the Zohar draws in the seeker of Truth, until chaotically consumed by the fire. The Zohar is the fourth and final level in the Tree of Life, commiserate with the fruit from the tree. I have plucked that succulent fruit from the Tree of Life; I have sliced and diced the fruit for easy consumption—now, I bring forth my effort to the reader with humility. Thank you for reading my book. Please do not read this book as a line, because the writing is not incrementally written; and please do not read this book as a circle, as if trying to persuade through repetition—rather, read my book as a spiral spinning in to a concluding point, allowing the vision to unwind inside your mind.

PART ONE
Chapter One

Sex and time are intertwined. In fact, Jewish Law encourages man to time his orgasm with his mate's orgasm by holding back his male energy during sex, trying to reach orgasm conjointly. Given the original sexual metaphor in the making of creation, an empty space pierced by a line of light delivering the seed of life, we should not be surprised to find a sexual component throughout creation, including the seven thousand year cycle dedicated to human history on planet Earth. As seen through the intrinsic structure refined from the Tree of Life planted upside down with roots pointed up into Heaven while the branches point down to the Earth. The Human Being mimics this design with our heads in the heavens and our body rooted in the ground.

The primordial seed cast by the Creator into the abyss grew into a tree whose fruits are scattered throughout creation. The Torah/Teaching of the Jewish People begins with an account of the first seven days of creation, relating to the seven lower parts from the Tree of Life known as, Zira Unpin/Small Faces is a prototype to the Seven Days of Creation and the subsequent seven thousand years, likened to seven chapters in a book. The creation of the first Human Being, who was originally made androgynous, is the genesis of the six thousand year calendar, beginning on the Sixth Day of Creation leading to the Seventh Day of Rest, celebrating woman. The time merging six into seven is known by the ancients as, The End of Days—end of the six thousand year male agenda.

In 1970, this original human calendar dating from the Sixth Day of Creation, reached 5730 years, the half-life of carbon-14, used in dating ancient artifacts. This demarcation line happening towards the end of the male cycle of six thousand years, left 260 years until the actual merging into woman, for the final Thousand Years of Woman and Peace. Those experiencing the Sixties high on hallucinogenic drugs unanimously gave witness to the end of something, by staging a huge party in Beth El, New York in 1969—Woodstock was the final spastic ejaculation beginning this long awaited transition from man to woman.

The Six Days of Creation, the prototype preparing man to ultimately merge with woman during this 260 year transitional juncture, is paramount to understanding the dramatic radical changes occurring in the world at this time. Each day of creation corresponds to a thousand years of subsequent history. The number 26 is the gematria of God's Ineffable Name YHVH. We are 26 thousand light years from the center of our galaxy, the Milky Way, the Sun appears to rotate around the North Star every 26,000 years and the Earth quakes every 26 seconds. From the four letters of the YHVH can be made the three tenses: היה/Past, הוה/Present and יהיה/Future.

The Sixth Day of Creation corresponding to the attributes of man, known by the term Yesod/Foundation, a term founded from the word Sod/Secret, is reflected in the human body as sex—the foundational secret to the Human Being. The sixth thousandth year in the human calendar began with the invention of the printing press seven hundred years ago. The printing press in that time was as revolutionary as the computer and internet in our time; both represent a transformational period caused by the sudden revelation of critical information—the time of Secret began seven centuries ago with the mechanical invention able to record, transmit and archive information, facts, data, figures, knowledge, details, evidence, findings, insight, intelligence, particulars, statistics, clues and wisdom.

We are presently at 2020 in Roman time, more than three quarters into this final phase of male development before officially merging with woman in 220 years, when the six thousand year calendar reaches completion. Three years ago, the eclipse of the Sun on August 21, 2017 on the cusp of Virgo, marked the inception to this transition between the waning male dominance and the rising Mayim Nukvim/Female Waters. The Roman Empire, as embodied in their two-thousand year Roman calendar, is the epitome of male energy expressed through religion and war, whose fulcrum is undeniably the United States of America.

War is a very male endeavor, as is the economy and the stuffing of religion down the throats of the unwilling. The wealth of America boggles the mind; gold buying pleasure instead of purpose—happiness has become the new spirituality, if you are happy you made it to heaven on Earth. This self-indulgent attitude is similar to a man having sex for his own Pleasure, a very Roman attitude demanding man's desire comes first. The first six thousand years of creation are dedicated to the completion of man, a man who will hold woman above himself, so woman can then crown the man.

To better understand the profound depth of sexuality, necessitates revisiting the original conceptual beginning of creation portrayed in the letter י/Yud (the first letter of the YHVH) resembling the opening at the end of the penis. This tiny letter with an accompanied value of ten is engraved into the quiescence radiance shinning out from the Creator, making a disturbance resulting in black holes. From the friction of the engraving twisting into the OreAinSof/LightWithoutEnd, a Hard Light, after a quarter million years, exploded into lines of liquid light suddenly stopped at the Command of the Creator. The Name Shaddai with a gematria of 314, the first three digits found at the head of an infinite array of random numbers known as pi, is the interloper between the line and the curve.

The beams of light shot forth from the black hole creating space also created time. Time and space have a symbiotic relationship since time is the measurement of motion through space happening because the Creator continually creates creation moment after moment. The nature of creation is not to be created, requiring a Creator to bring the potential into actuality, the same pattern exist each moment, moving creation bit by bit through a slight juxtaposition. Without the constant support of the Creator creating moment by moment, all of creation would melt back into the abyss of nothing because the nature of creation is not to exist.

The ubiquitous invocation of God's Name during sex is witness to the intense connection between the Creator and creation because sex is completely beyond logic. The essential elements to sex are Will and Pleasure, the two most chaotic human abilities, laid bare during sex, as naked desire. Only the Human Being can be naked. The concept of nudity traces back to the original foreskin coving the letter י/Yud at the end of the penis. *And man was embarrassed, so he hid himself.* Women wear clothes for a different reason than men. Women wear clothes to shield or enhance the form of their bodies. Men ware clothes to hide.

Since man produces sperm through his eyes, the engineered curves and contours of woman designed by the Creator induces desire, since man is often seduced by what he sees. Thus, men are always looking at women, who in turn are constantly concerned about their looks. Women are more vulnerable to what they hear, thereby being easily seduced by voice or the softly spoken words murmuring promises and lies. Women are more malleable than men because their objective in sex is to get the sperm; woman are nonjudgmental doing whatever is needed to draw the energy down—her enticement to him. The body of woman is more important to the man but the energy of man is more important to the woman. The more the man hold's back his sexual urge to explode out, the greater is his energy and the more righteous is his state of being.

Ejaculation is compared to the arrow and the bow. The further back the string of the bow is drawn, the further forward and with more vitality is the arrow shot forth. This same paradigm is engaged at the onset of creation causing infinite arrows of light suddenly stopped then turned into dots of stars before reverberating into broken waves in a tempestuous sea moving at the speed of light. It was in this cosmic soup, a composite of primordial liquid, that the Earth was conceived and life began. The first human being was made from water and clay kneaded together to form a body then the soul, made from fire and air, was blown into the nose of the Adom to give him life.

The reason for creation was to create a Human Being with freedom of choice so God can be known in low. But first, the Human Being had to be assessed. So, God took the soul of the Adom, male and female, to the Garden of Eden to test the man, leaving the physical body to roam the Earth as the human animal devoid of a human soul. Meanwhile, the soul is taken to outer rim of the solar system where, in the Garden of Eden man is told not eat from the Tree of Life, least he relinquish his soul back to the Creator.

Once in the Garden of Eden, woman was taken from within man. He loved her at once. Having seen all the animal with mates, now he too had a mate. Wanting to protect his mate, Adom told her, Eating from the Tree of Life or even touching the Tree of Life will bring on death. Subsequently, the Serpent came, saw the two having sex and wanted the woman. Later, the Serpent engaged the woman in speech and eventually pushed her against the Tree of Life. She did not die. The man became suspect in the woman's eyes because he had lied to her, saying she would die if she touched the tree, enticing her to eat the fruit.

Maybe, she thought the Serpent was right, because the fruit opened her eyes. She gave the fruit to the man who also eat and his eyes also opened. Later, God asked them, Why did you eat from the Tree of Life? The man said, The woman gave the fruit to him, so eat it; the women said, The snaked tricked her—the Serpent had nothing to say, but as a result would have to go legless, eating the dust from the ground. God rebuked man for being weak and wiping his hands on the woman. Then asked the woman why she gave the fruit to the man?

The woman admitted, she did not want to die and the man marry another woman, so she poisoned him with the fruit. The man was weak and the woman was vindictive. God wanted to kill the man right then but the man repented what he had done, so God gave the man a thousand years of life to return to the Earth and begin the six thousand year process of picking up the sparks which had fallen, as a result of the man's actions in the Garden of Eden. So, with his newly forged foreskin, man returned to the Earth from where he was made, a 130 years later to unite with his woman.

In those first years, the main vocation of man was to have sex with his woman. Each man was born with at least one mate. The great pleasure visited upon man in the Garden of Eden was reenacted over and over to ensure later generations. The human animal merged the knowledge of survival into modern man. Now, that there was man, now there was sex and a lot of sex. Fifteen hundred years later, because the world was covered with sperm, even on rocks and trees, the Creator decided to bring a flood and clean everything up after these first ten extraordinary generations.

Every human being is a composite of the human animal combine with the human soul, often times in opposition. The body wants sex to procreate but the soul wants sex to get closer to God because the androgynous nature of the unified Human Being is meant to meld into the Oneness of the Creator. Each person is a blend of these qualities harboring unique capabilities. Truly, everyone is a genius but few find their true trade in life. What makes the Human Being different from the animal is our ability to articulate thoughts into words and to practice freedom of choice.

There is no bigger challenge to man than the urge to be sexual. Man learns at an early age how to calm male sexual ambitions by diverting the mind, which seems odd at first glance. I mean, what malfunction ties together the mind and the penis? The mind is tied to every part of the body which reacts like an obedient servant except the penis which seems to have a mind of his own, getting hard at inappropriate times. To better understand this phenomenon we must delve into the esoteric meaning of the number 666.

Chapter Two

The six is the last number and the final point of the two overlaid triangles representing the human torso plus the five limbs: two arms and two legs. Sex is number six. Sex is a third way we differ from the animal who has sex merely to procreate at naturally appointed times, whereas the human being can be sexual anytime, plus human sexual expression is rarely the same. The sex and the mind are inexorably tied together into one composite ubiquitous expression into—Oh my God. The overwhelming experience of sex reduces the most hardened individual into ecstasy.

There is a logical explanation how and why God fits into the equation of sex, mind and mouth. In the Hebrew language, man is called איש/Ish and woman is called אשה/Isha, the difference being, one has the letter ה/Hey and the other the letter י/Yud. When put together, the י/Yud and the ה/Hey make the Name, יה/Ya, the first of the Seven Names. It should be noted: before God, all sexual acts are permitted; however people show their love to each other is without judgment—God loves people having sex. So, if people love sex and God loves sex, then what's the problem?

The final sixth point in the two overlaid triangles representing the human body is a conglomerate from the first five points, all struggling to find quiescence in their final iteration just prior to being revealed. When people gather to witness an event, the pushing stops when the event actually begins. Sex is no different. The five different components comprising sex push their influence into the sexual experience, yet at climax, all stands still awaiting the affluence of the brain transported down the spin, cooked into the balls then delivered into a forceful ejaculation pulsing with emotions.

The first emotion is kindness housed in the right arm close to the lungs breathing air into the body. The movement associated with kindness is opening, giving to all without discrimination because the nature of kindness is to give. Kind people become frustrated, even angry when they can not give. A man, who is exemplarily in giving becomes depressed over impotency, the most intense kind of giving. It is well known, a man would give away everything if not for his woman. The impetus to give is at the very nature of man, epitomizing his desire for woman.

The second emotion, housed in the left arm close to the heart, is severity. The necessity to hold back is an essential ability to sex. To overcome the intense desire to give, the ability to hold back through contraction must be even greater than the desire to give. Contraction squeezes together in an attempt to contain, consolidating energy for later use. These two harlequin skills, one revealed and the other hidden are the basis for all that follows. These two end points, giving and receiving, hold between their arms the diverse possibilities available for human interaction. The balance between giving and receiving during sex is a dance of emotions and spontaneous inspiration.

The third emotion, corresponding to the torso, is the combination of giving and holding back, representing beauty, truth and peace. Beauty is imperfect because two can never become one; it is the closeness to unity which is beautiful, not the perfection—the impatient friction from disparity is the nectar of love. Shalom/Peace also means Complete. The integration of white and red, of fire and water, of man and woman happens continually within each person producing a true emotion, the completion of a process produces the first triangle. The triangle is the first true geometric expression of completion, without which peace does not exist.

The second triangle is a refraction from the prior triangle of emotion replicated into action. The right leg steps out and forward, an affirmative action into the world. This attribute of action, known by the concept of Victory, is connected to infinity through the emptying of all resources to achieve final triumph. This male energy invoked in man to compete, to fight, to be dedicated to a cause animates man. The foot, though furthest from the head, actually touches the ground, another difference between the Human Being who stands erect with the head commanding the heart while the animal goes on all fours.

The fifth aspect to the lower triangle is the left leg stepping back, known as Hod/Splendor, beauty arising from modesty, comparable to the setting of the sun or the mystical magic of the Moon from where comes mensuration, the ultimate expression of female holding back. The left leg powers the right leg when working in unison, thus the saying, Behind every successful man is strong woman. These two bi-polar qualities of the Human Being in emotion and action are the extremities tied to the truth in the torso of each human body. They are called extremities because they are not essential.

Lastly, the sixth element of the two triangles is sex. Male sex is exposed: the two testicles and the penis, whereas female sex is the opposite: the vagina and the two ovaries—both representing the three of aspects of the triangle. Male sex is made to give while female sex is made to receive. Each are fitted for life; one to produce the male seed while the other produces the female egg—the sexual components for conception. The orgasm is the ultimate reward for plowing and planting. Sex has a direct positive effect in Heaven, as is known, The greater the pleasure, the deeper the soul is touched.

This lower point from the two overlaid triangles is the culmination of all energies produced by the body coalescing in sex, to drive home the DNA being spontaneously produced inside the brain of the man. Men can produce sperm from the time of puberty until old age. Woman are the opposite, having a short time, often only a few decades to be of childbearing ability. The man spontaneously produces myriads of sperm in one ejaculation while woman is born with a few thousand eggs, to be dropped once a month for perhaps thirty years out of her life.

Man and woman while having sex are combining the infinite and the finite coming together in joyous rectification as the line of man and the curve of woman through the magic of Shadai and Pi momentarily melding into one flesh, yielding a spontaneous sexual experience, unique from all other human exploits or ordeals. Only childbirth magnifies the energy of sex, an experience relegated only to women. The entire sexual process is connoted through the number six. The 666 is 18 equaling the gematria of the word ʼn/Chai/Life; six times six is 36, twice Chai/Life—life's elixir is Pleasure. Nothing stands before Will's desire for Pleasure.

All the ins and outs, the ups and downs that have happened throughout history are culminating in our time, The End of Days, the end of the six thousand year calendar preceding the Thousand Years of Woman and Peace. The orgasm has begun and those trying to rest control over the thing, good luck, because nothing stands before Will's desire for Pleasure; money and power are meaningless before the fountain of life—where nothing enters in, is where God enters. Sex is a triangle between the man, the woman and the Creator, exemplified in the six thousand year calendar leading to culmination.

Sexual metaphor permeates creation on every level, particularly in historic context. The rise and fall of empires; the looting, the rampant raping—produces war and the spoils of war. Sex is a type of warfare where one is victorious while the other is conquered. There are those who eagerly spread their legs when the conqueror comes and there are those who resist but eventually succumb because all is obliterated by the force of sex encompassed in the number six made from two triangles, the male and the female interlocked.

A man who forces his way into woman is a rapist; a man who seduces his way into woman is a thief—but he who is invited in, is a lover. Much of human history records the rapes and the plundering of peoples, accelerating the mixing of the races. Also, history abounds with trade between nations, each seducing the other with their natural resources. Yet, the culmination of history is undoubtedly love. When sex and love combine, the doors to the Garden of Eden open; the greater the Pleasure the further in we go—where God is elusive, but waiting.

Six is the culmination of the three vertical pillars upon which is hung the two triangles embodying the torso, arms, legs and sex. Everything prior to sex is internal; sex is the first outer expression from an internal process—what exudes from male sex is the final synthesis of the human experience condensed into a single seed, the smallest cell in the body. The egg from the woman is the largest cell in the body; the man can release infinite amounts of sperm in a lifetime while woman is born with a few thousand eggs—together they produce the spiral of life called the DNA extracted from the line of the man and the circle of the woman.

Each thousand year period in the six thousand year calendar corresponding to the Six Days of Creation has a highpoint culminating around the year 666, the sign of sexual prowess and arousal. Each thousand year intervals has a 666 and corresponding climactic event. In the first occasion of 666 was during time of Enoch who was taken by God at 365 years to be the Angle of the Earth called Metatron, instead of the customary thousand year limit for that era,. The year 666 was when the Mayan calendar was first conceived, with an expiration date of 5,106 years into the future or 2012 in Roman time.

A new human paradigm was conceived during the first instance of the 666. In the second iteration of the 666 in the year 1666, the great flood came. Considered a wet dream by the Talmud, wiping out all terrestrial life with the exception of Noah his wife Alma and their three sons plus their wives. These eight people were left to populate the world from the accumulated genetic history produced from the previous generations, creating a new, more moderate version of man. In each thousand year segment, the time of the 666 was always a turning point in history. The final iteration of 666 was in 5666 or 1906. One week before New Year 5666, Einstein published $E=MC^2$ the secret to light.

The year 1906 was also a time of great creativity Europe where Modern Art celebrated the many permutations of form acclaimed in cubism. There is only one place to go after the conclusion of the 666 and that is the 777, a number predominate in our time. Trump was elected in the year 5,777 and when inaugurated he was seventy years, seven months and seven days. On March 11, 2020 when the World Health Organization announced Covid-19 a pandemic, there were 7,770,000,000 people in the world. The End of Days, which began in 1970 is where the 666 faces off with the 777 as they collide in our time, causing the long awaited paradigm shift.

Each of the 22 Hebrew letters is affixed with a number called gematria but the inverse is also true from the side of the Creator where each letter was originally a number value, later to be translated into words of prophesy. The power of 666 is diffused throughout creation and every person alive on the Earth is part of this cosmic coitus. Each generation is part of this process, coming in and going out hoping for completion, but now the time has come for culmination. God has been waiting for us but after fifty years of intense tribulation and birth pangs, now is the time to push out the birth and change the world forever.

Chapter Three

In 1998, which is three times 666, the world was hit with a blast from a neutron star for an unprecedented five minutes knocking out satellites and earthbound instrumentation precisely five years to the day before the planet Mars would come closest to the Earth, ever on August 27, 2003. Two years and two days later on August 29, 2005 after the martian close encounter, Katrina storms in to New Orleans destroying the allusion that America is beautiful. While the world watched, the poorer populous of the city was left abandoned, huddled in a stadium or shot for looting. America, the only superpower left standing, showed herself to be an immoral country run by autocrats for the money. While starving looters were being shot, the government was looting the treasury of the nation for a war which could never be won but would make the wealthy far wealthier. Bush in Hebrew means, Embarrassment. Two thousand years ago the Midrash predicted, The last King of Rome would be called Irom/Naked because of the embarrassment he will bring to his people by robbing the treasury for the sake his religion. The Pope celebrated this time by going to Israel in 1999 and starting another Intifada/Upraising by demanding a Palestinian State.

At the same time as the Earth was being blasted by a nuclear star in 1998, three times 666 (Bill Gates added a senior to his name so it will equal 666 in ASCII script in 1998). Rome was exploding with arrogance, with a number directly depicting sex. Bill Clinton received a blow job in the Oval Office of the White House in 1998 from a Jewish intern on her knees, as the Talmud reminds us, When Jews go down, Rome goes up. This arrogant act, because the Oval Office belongs to all American citizens, influenced the Creator to speak to the world through a series of names, revealing a new take on history. Because God wants to be known in low, and there is nothing lower than sex, as exclaimed by Martin Luther the pioneer of Lutherism some centuries ago, We are born between shit and piss. Where ever we go, God goes with us wanting to be known in low. The Free Love of the Sixties came from young people saying, they could not wait to marry to have sex because the atomic bomb was threatening to eliminate life. Rome exploited love for unrestrained sex.

After the culmination of the two thousand years of Rome, the mantle was passed to George Bush and Dick Cheney, who counseled with their close advisers, Colin Powell and Condoleezza Rice, nicknamed Cunti. These four, Bush, Dick, Colin and Cunti, fucked up the world and after one term ran against John Kerry. The word Kerry in Hebrew means, Wet dream. Bush and Dick won and continued their nefarious deeds for another four years before being replaced by President Obama. Nonetheless, John Boehner, whose name is properly pronounced "boner," was left as the Speaker of the House sticking it to the president until eventually he got small and slipped away. President Obama's eight years ended with Weiner spilling the beans to Comey. The election of Donald Trump, with his ejaculatory personality, is the obvious fulfillment of male determination, poised to enact the orgasmic outcome upon the waiting world. But in the end, proved himself to be no more than a weak, premature ejaculation. Just another thief and illegitimate leader. God speaks the world in the language of the world but no one seems to be listening or watching. The world has yet to learn how to connect the dots because we are constantly being fed disinformation.

The last hundred years from 5666/1906 to 2006/5766 constituted the end of warfare; though war continues, the calamity of the stormed named Katrina (Keter/Crown is denoted by Chaos) followed by the economic collapse was blowback from God. After the initial fall of Rome from the 9/11 attacks, directly after achieving two thousand years, was a sign. I watched the Towers fall over and over but only saw the fall of Rome. However, Rome refused to go quietly into the night while they still held the lever of power. By 2012, the year the 26,000 year Mayan calendar ended as we traversed the galactic horizon facing the center of the galaxy the world cried out for peace. In terms of giving birth, this is dilation but in terms of sexuality, when women is most open. Rome is the quintessential male prowess whose sun is quickly setting while a new man arises. Dogma can no longer stem the tide of truth coming like a tsunami; the religious believe, Trump was sent by God has come true but not in the manner in which religion had expected—Trump is the 777, good in casinos but not in life.

A calendar without an ending point is a depressing reality tortured by the steady incremental pace into atrophy. A calendar with a precise beginning and end, generally is tied to some natural phenomenon. The five thousand year Mayan calendar follows the path around the North Star; the six thousand year calendar adapted by the Jewish People focuses around the week, the month and the year following both the Sun and the Moon. The Mayan calendar begins 666 years into the Hebrew calendar and ends at dilation announcing the time has come for birth. Nothing can determine the precise moment of birth because the process is mainly controlled by the stars in conjunction with Mother Earth, who is also giving birth to a new era. The Earth is cracking open, icecaps melt falling into the sea to later be vomited up as storms inundating dry land where half of America is on fire while the other half is underwater. Earthly birth is breaking the chains of servitude from masterminds trying to hold back the force of nature, as Mother Earth writhes in her birth pangs. In the six thousand year calendar, the year 2012 was 5772; seventy-two is the highest number referring to the Human Being with the gematria of Chesed/Kindness.

World birth is happening. The last generation of Rome has arisen proclaiming, There is nothing spiritual in religion. Also science, the other bastion of Roman propagating with their Big Bang Theory where creation comes out of nothing but eventually after 13 billion light years of time, turns into something—life on planet Earth replete with a perfect eclipse of the Sun by the Moon, as if to say, this perfect geometric happening was prearranged by the Creator. War, religion, politics and money are all male endeavors devouring the Earth on the precipice of extinction. Caught between religion and science, the Human Being has been easily manipulated, made to crave worthless things satisfying their imposed addiction, spurning them to buy more and more until life is cluttered with useless objects blocking the spiritual light from entering into the human experience. While the world's attention has been diverted by pictures from space and upheavals on the Earth, the real story dances right before our eyes, but who is watching? The culmination of six thousand years is happening, day by day, hour by hour yet the news is full of politics and entertainment.

According to our galactic schedule, the end of the six thousand year male agenda, a quasi birth-sexual affair has come to conclusion. Time is spiraling in, going faster and faster towards the fulcrum where birth and orgasm will happen together; logic and proper decorum is expendable during birth and sex—now is the time for action. As the leading consumer in the world, America will never go back to her gluttonous ways and addictive attitudes, instead she will adapt to what is needed and change according to the situation. The East is more adaptable than the West, obvious from their oral language which stretches the vowel to achieve a new meaning, whereas in the West, changes in the consonants determines the meaning of the word. Human beings are similar to one another but none are the same, languages also are similar in our ability to articulate thoughts into words; similarly, continents and countries are different and diverse from each other. The Earth with her seven continents and three oceans, is configured in the form of the Tree of Life, like the human body made of three triangles and the power of speech. For the body to function in a productive coordinated manner, melding all aspects of the body into one, diversity is necessary.

The Earth, like the body, was created for Pleasure since Pleasure is the elixir of life. Birth and sex are Pleasure to an extreme, since both are founded in the fountain of heavenly sustenance. Every time man and women have sex, something is born; when man and man have sex, nothing is born—not physical nor spiritual, but love lives engraved into the heavenly firmament, forever. Other than Jewish men, man on man sex is permitted along with all other types of sexual expression. Women with other women are completely exempt from any law, since what they do is not deemed sexual. History is laden with mistakes strewn about in examples of human dictates upsetting the natural order of things. Both science and religion are major polluters of Truth, both are guilty of the same crime, making assumptions based on spurious fact. Everything in existence, exists because the Creator is constantly creating, since the nature of creation is, not to be. Creation needs to be brought out of nothing into something moment by moment. Without constant maintenance, all of existence would fall back into the abyss of oblivion. This concept of constant creation can be seen in the sine-wave. Crossing the zero point relegates the energy into nothing from where a new wave begins in the opposite direction. For this reason, the 26,000 Mayan calendar is divided into two 13,000 years cycles.

Energized by the Creator a step ahead of the past, the burgeoning future accomplishes the feat of motion as measured by time. Nothingness is where God inserts the dot of life to bring about the next half cycle of the circle displaced by the movement of time thus causing motion to occur in the form of the sine wave—all life moves with this same rhythm modulated by the Human Being applying their free Will into each and every atom in the body to do an action upon the Earth. What the Human Being engraves into the Earth is written in Heaven, each person inscribed into the Book of Life. The Roman calendar treats life as if time is a straight line extending into infinity, but this assumption is blatantly wrong. As seen by the spiraling time cycles in the ancient calendars with exact beginning and exact ends, like the Hebrew and Mayan calendars, time cycles. By synchronizing these three calendars particularly around the half-life of carbon-14 at the end of the Sixties in 5730/1970 brings clarity to a world consumed by unfounded errant assumptions.

Science looks upon creation with incremental vision, following the line extending until achieving atrophy, since all lines must end. However, the circle in the cycle of life never ends, just keeps getting closer the source, the Creator of creation. The cyclical nature of our planet, like the cyclical nature of woman, is tethered to the Moon. Man's arc is much wider, going around the Sun. The male linear line of life is coming to conclusion as the transformation between the line of incremental thinking dissolves into the circle where the Thousand Years of Woman and Peace is resides. When the line and circle combine into one, a spiral is momentarily manufactured. The spiral of life is found everywhere from the solar system to the galaxy, from the plants to the DNA, everything cycles included time; therefore, history also cycles, forced into allotted confines of time—a story divided into chapters.

An illustration of a cyclical way of viewing history is the ancient six thousand year calendar, prototype to the six thousand years of human history upon planet Earth; each thousand years is an individual circle of time coming to climax around the number 666—the orgasm in each thousand year segment. In the first thousand year segmentation, corresponding to the attribute of Chesed/Kindness, the Human Being lived to a thousand years, plus life abounded everywhere on the Earth exemplifying this first attribute. However, on the second thousand year segment, the attribute of Gevorah/Severity, at the juncture of 1666, the great flood came and destroyed all life with the exemption of Noah and his three sons, their wives plus two of each animal as not to lose the genetic code to life. The third thousand year period, begins with Avraham coming to the Earth from the Tower of Babel in the year two thousand, starting the two thousand years of teaching when amazing spiritual teachers descend to the Earth, seeded throughout the globe. At the end of the these two thousand years of teaching, precisely 120 years before the scheduled end, Rome destroys the last hope of the future in Israel then sends the Jewish People to be exiled into every part of the world.

The thousand years of Hod/Retreat begins with the Catholic Church and their Crusades into the Middle East ending with the Black Plague which wiped out as many Christians as the Crusade had laid waste to the Muslims and Jews. The Jews in between Islam and Christianity were lost in the exile, wearing black, studying Torah, making communities around the world tied together by the Oral Torah having been written down at the advent of the exile. Great teachers, geniuses arose squeezing new knowledge from the old words because the cauldron of life made them sweat, producing this new knowledge from each generation according to the time ticking away the years until the new age would arrive. We are presently 780 years into that new age celebrated at the inception as the Renascence, also known, according to the Tree of Life, as the time of Yesod/Foundation from the word Sod/Secret, when all the secrets of creation are being revealed. The Zohar/Brilliance, is the greater light coming forth from the darkness; written by a talmudic figure, Rabbi Shimmon ben Yichoi two thousand years ago, was channeled down the Earth seven hundred years ago; a thousand years prior to merging into the Thousand Years of Woman and Peace.

The Zohar was meant for the End of Days, meaning the end of the six thousand year male agenda. Yet, this obscure text written in ancient Aramaic and Hebrew, even deciphered into the modern language still remains abstruse. However, over the last few centuries, the light from the Zohar has penetrated into the minds of men. A few centuries after the initial writing of the Zohar in Spain, the Ari came to the town of Sfat in Northern Israel, taught for three years then died a young man but his scribe, Chaim Vital, wrote 13 books attributed to his master's words, known to the world as, Cabala/Receive, the most feminine of all the teachings. The elevated words of the Cabala were assimilated into Europe where great hidden Masters of the Name transmitted this sacred and deep knowledge to the simple people by means of metaphor and stories known as Chasidut. After ten generations, the Zohar is now available to all peoples in various languages—yet up until now, the Zohar remains aloof, unpredictable and inexplicable. Why was the Zohar was written for this time just prior to the advent of the Thousand Years of Woman and Peace?

Chapter Four

In the three hundred years between the emergence of the Zohar and the subsequent key to this knowledge embedded in the Cabala, the first printing press was invented accelerating the movement of information by which the world is latticed together. This sudden exponential change, escalated the flow of knowledge, expediting progress for the betterment of society. The Holy Roman Catholic Church, who rightly identified the 666 as sexual energy through the dogma of their teachings, made sex immoral and censured from books. This cloak of darkness spread throughout the world along with their dogma: Jews killed god, Black People are cursed to be slaves and homosexual are despised in God's Eyes. These oppositional attitudes to the natural flow of life has challenged the human spirit. The Holy Roman Catholic Church is the root of religion; real spiritual traditions adopt religion to get tax-free ownership of property, forever—plus, the ability to remain anonymous and undisclosed in all investigations. The partner to religion is science. Religion is adamant while science is forever changing according to their relativity. Religion and science are the two extremities to the boundaries of common thought. Thinking outside the box of those strict boundaries is heresy, causing social repudiation.

The printed word was filtered through two apertures; science provided facts plus an uninformed interpretation, while religion gave exact directions explained only by the adherence to dogma. This inevitable cloak of darkness with which Rome conquered the world came with an antidote to be revealed at the final decline of Rome, the Zohar. The reason why the Zohar was meant for our time is precisely because, the darkness brought on by these illegitimate pronouncements had extinguished all light. Literally, the word Zohar means Brilliance, a light commiserate with the darkness. The illumination of the Zohar answers the ancient question, Where is the Creator? The ancient view of creation was, Everything was created by the Creator, but they assumed, the Creator had created creation then left the workings of creation in the nimble hands of the stars and constellations. As a result from this assumption, people interacted with the stars instead of praying to the Creator, eventually turning starlight into magic. The Zohar is a map of creation coming forth from the black hole, creating a galaxy, solar system and a fecund Earth built from a pebble found at the foot of Merkavah/Chariot.

Because this sublime knowledge could only be corroborated once telescopes were employed and satellites launched, so the scope and form of creation could be discovered, only then could the Zohar be properly understood. The Zohar was left until the End of Days to be revealed as proof, the ancients had a better grasp on reality than do the technicians of our time. Life is a collusion between body and spirit. Only by seeing beyond the dictates of Rome, can the world embrace the beautiful future. The Zohar cuts through the darkness revealing the truth, the configuration of the Tree of Life replicated throughout creation then coming to finality in the Human Being with the uncanny ability to articulate thoughts into speech and thereby go beyond instinct. However, this process defined by form also has the component of time woven within the Tree of Life. Time is predicated on the lower seven elements of the ten components to the Tree of Life, two triangles plus speech erupting from the empty space made within the three sides of the triangles. These seven מדות/Measures, as they are known, correspond to music and emotions.

The major difference between Heaven and Earth is witnessed through corporeal erosion; the mountains eventually crumble to dust, water evaporates into wind to be sacrifice to the Sun—but Heaven is forever. Therefore, time is a worldly function to which the heavens must adapt. God wants to be known in low, the original impetus for creation, but there is a time limit to this desire and the time is running out. The Six Days of Creation, prototype to these six thousand years of male domination will come to a close in 220 years when the calendar reaches six thousand. Time is based on disintegration. The most rigorous method examining time is carbon-14 testing, whose half-life is 5730 or 1970 when the sixties ended with three days in the mud at the Woodstock gathering in Bethel, New York in the summer of 1969. Unbeknownst to everyone, the Human Being had achieved the half-life of carbon-14 after 5730 years of our species on this planet. Carbon-14 is produced in the upper atmosphere at the same rate carbon-14 disintegrates on the Earth. In 1970, the original amount of carbon-14 invested in the first Human Being halved, beginning the last 260 years, the End of Days.

The carbon-14 calendar and the five thousand year Mayan calendar overlaid on the six thousand year ancient human calendar, beginning with first man, shows a pattern consistent with the lower six components to the Tree of Life coming to conclusion in this time. These three calendars represent: the body, the seed and the pregnancy. Half the atoms in the human body are carbon; the six thousand years made from two triangles produces the seed—the pregnancy begins 666 years after the creation of man. The due date is 5,106 years in the future: the winter of 2012 when the galaxy opened in dilation while the Earth passed through the galactic horizon. After a seemingly 13,000 year orbit around the North Star (Our solar system does not actually make a circle around the North Star, it only appears that way) the Mayan calendar ended. The Earth has entered into the time of birth when faith in the human spirit is vital, when clarity is revealed and when the time has come to push. The introduction of Covid-19 came as a sign, the birth is imminent therefore activity halted and focus fell on the Human Being to show love to each other through the simple gesture of wearing a mast.

The prior five thousand years became as foreplay before sex but now, after 780 years of sexual history, the long awaited cosmic ejaculation is about to happen but suddenly someone farted, polluted the air and made it hard to breathe. The body stopped undulating long enough to feel the hot sweat on the slippery flesh and realize, the corporeal had overtaken the soul. The Sixties ended with an orgy of drugs, sex and rock&roll; fifty years later, those same people and their children, are addicted to money, gorging themselves with equity and liquidity, evicting millions from their homes, so they can have more. Before the ejaculation, there is a time of immobility when both the man and woman know something is coming from somewhere far away yet inexplicably present with anticipation building from its own accord, pushing away all obstacles through the explosive nature of orgasm to come forth vindicating the struggle to bring this energy out of Heaven while God is being vocalized in an erratic prayer of flesh melding with soul in ecstatic bliss. In the year 2020 or 5780, the Earth stopped and the world is waiting.

There are two types of orgasm. The male orgasm explodes through the man like liquid conveyed by a pipe, while woman orgasm is molten lead coming up from the Earth. The goal of sexuality is to orgasm together. This sexual standard is relevant to world history as a bar set high by which to evaluate our goals. In a world made by the Creator to give pleasure to the Human Being, events are meant to serve both man and woman equally, yet they get pleasure differently. Man is more focused on Heaven while woman is dedicated to the Earth. The difference between Heaven and Earth are many and diverse but the rate of change is the most ubiquitous. Because the Earth is constantly disintegrating, change chases life into the grave; a short time to make a mark into the corporeal which is quickly eradicated by the winds of time blowing everything into oblivion—to live in the moment is the most satisfying but also the most dangerous. Animals live in the moment but Human Beings look to the future, trying to fix a trajectory to a hypothetical goal, perhaps decades in the future.

Curiously, the Human Being has the ability to throw a projectile and hit a target through our ability to extrapolate into the future, similar to our ability to articulate thoughts into speech through the mechanism of the three triangles: head, body and lower body. The tenth component to the Tree of Life is woman who exemplifies speech, an ability also requiring extrapolation into the future to complete a sentence or convey an idea. Whereas, the other nine attributes to the Tree of Life are either male, female or a combination, the tenth and final expression comes through the lips of Woman, characterized as birth and speech. In the seventh and final thousand year segment, beginning in 220 years, when Earth will give birth as the whole world speaks with one voice. Different from the animals, the Human Being needs to be aware of the future while living in the moment. Another unusual aspect to the Human Being is our erect stature, with head looking towards the heavens while the feet are upon the ground, whereas the animal goes on all fours continually staring at the ground. Man is the conduit between Heaven and Earth but woman is Earth, as in Mother Earth. The male/female paradigm is constantly falling in and out of balance but the ultimate goal is ultimately to satisfy woman.

In the construct of the Torah/Teaching of the Jewish People, women are exempt from time oriented positive commandments since her profound connection with the Earth renders her own time. Time is measured by Earth's erosion, yet each thousand year segment produces at different rate. For example, in the first thousand years, life was expansive with people living close to a thousand years. Even time was accelerated; events taking eons in our time, happened regularly back then—a thousand years of unimpeded exponential growth was followed by a thousand years of human arrogance ending in the Noah's Flood. In 666 of the first thousand year segment, conception happened with a due date five thousand years in the future, the winter of 2012 when the Earth lined up with center of the galaxy causing a galactic dilation in preparation for birth. When birth occurs, the direct sustenance connected to the abdomen through the umbilical cord is severed, as the eyes see and the mouth opens strident with voice. This same birth process has been at play in the world for centuries of history portending to a specific time within this millennium all with the unbeknownst final goal fixed into the future where the Thousand Years of Woman and Peace await.

The perfidy of history written by the victor is a malicious way to skew the truth to the purpose of domination. Real history is the memory stored in the DNA, a generational mind trying to remember the truth; each generation striving to find their way along the darkened path from where the past skirts into the underbrush—while the illuminated road manufactured by malicious minds wants to exploit life instead of living life. Those with money and vast resources miss out on life because they are able to buy their reality based on a skewed history of the past. But, opulence has not brought happiness or peace to the world, only subjugation of the free spirit, rendering the world boring. The lower two triangles comprising man are the six parameters of space: up and down, front and back, left and right. Woman, the seventh and final attribute, is time imbedded in conclusion. All actions are relegated to the inextricable conclusion into what can be construed as God Time. God never changes. The plot of this six thousand year story is immutable and about to be revealed as the conclusion draws close, the Truth is being extricated from the phony and false arbitrators using money and power to obstruct what is real.

Chapter Five

The brain is furthest from sex yet the mind is indispensable to sex. According to the Torah/Teaching of the Jewish People, man can not achieve an erection without engaging the center of the mind, called Dat/Knowing. Therefore the pronouncement from the first sexual act as described in the Torah, And man knew woman. Seemingly, a man knows the woman before they have sex, not during sex. To better understand the connection from brain to penis is necessary to first understand the nature of this third and highest triangle composing the Tree of Life. The mind thinks with the two hemispheres of the brain but knowing happening in the center. The two lower intertwining triangles composing the six measures of emotions point down, but the upper triangle of intellect in the head sometimes points down adding knowing to the emotions and sometimes faces up into Heaven drawing down inspiration. This peculiar aspect of the Human Being is commonly known as the Third Eye, the defining human attribute causing both bliss and heartbreak beyond what any animal can experience. Animals have their genesis in the previous world where acceptance is natural and pain is experience differently than human pain.

The erect Human Being was constructed from the dust of the Earth to where we will eventually return; the Human Being is unique in the universe, able to freely chose between good and bad—with our power to know. Without knowing there is no judgment, no reward and no punishment, life becomes instinctual and without purpose. Knowing is an experience producing consciousness from the time we are born into this world until the last breath. There is no physical third eye yet it is widely assumed the third eye is situated in the middle of the forehead opposite the cerebellum/Little Brain buried deep it the back of the skull. The cerebellum is responsible for coordinating voluntary movements, including motor skills such as balance, coordination, and posture. An infant child reaches for a flame, the experience is burned into the brain thereby classified as knowledge. The consternation between the logic of the brain and the consciousness of Knowing is a constant reminder to the mind while wheeling free choice. The integration of mind over body is a continual challenge from newborn to old age. Truly, every moment of consciousness is a struggle to extend the line of thought into action.

There is no greater action than the act of sex when Knowing reaches zenith. The tip of the intellect points up into the unknown and unknowable apex of will, drawing down a light obliterating logic, pushing away constraints, wanting only to be known. Sex begins in the mind of man, woman has a totally different process relaying more on emotions than mind. The essential difference between man and woman is found in their opposite directions. Man points up. He is the conduit from Heaven while woman who points down because she is the receptor for what is coming from Heaven to Earth. Together the Human Being, male and female, synthesize the physical and spiritual to produce the next generation. There will always be rich and there will always be poor because we are meant to give love to each other, helping with the process of life. This process is done naturally through sex with overwhelming joy and pleasure, the precise reality the Creator wanted for our planet. No wonder the first action taken by man and woman when initially divided into gender, was to have sex, a deeply unique nuanced experience. From the beginning of creation when the Creator implanted a beam of light into an empty space causing all of creation to be imbued with sexual metaphor, sex became the language of creation. Man and woman are the final iteration from the initial inspiration within the Mind of God.

Certainly, God has no mind or body parts. God adopted the sexual language of creation which is embedded within the construct of formation. There are seven chapters in the story of creation. Chapter six, the last thousand year segment in the six thousand year male agenda concludes with man merging into woman. But something is wrong because history is not full of love. History is filthy with ego, repugnant with rape, a world bereft of real joy and pleasure, plus the litter from the past is constantly pushing into the future. The people of the world comprise the undulating skin of our planet writhing with life sensitive to touch electric with feeling longing for sensation. We are a naked people scantily veiled in clothes grown from the ground, living in houses hewed into mountains or open on the plains. We walk on the dirt, float on the water and glide in the air; the Earth expresses a vibration filtered through the planets before being spoken into the universe by Pluto's five moons in elliptical orbits representing the five parts of speech: throat, pallet, tongue, teeth and lips.

The Earth is pulsating with the human spirit, crawling with animals, growing with plants all immersed in a flush of air carried by streams of mist continually watering the terrain and filling the oceans. But, after six millennium of sex, the body is sweaty with exertion and the fetid air smells with an odd odor from flesh being melded together by the constant insistent, pounding of progress to accelerate. The question is, what is man's intention? It is then we realized, we're being fucked. Of all the words torn from the body then used to revile one another like, asshole, prick, cunt, etc. none so profound like the word Fuck, which is a verb indicating action. If sex is the middle rung of the ladder to Heaven; love is the higher rung—fucking is the lowest rung. Fucking happens when the mind intrudes into sex from an aloof uninvolved place manipulating the other person. The sheath around the stream of white light coming out of the soul is made from the chaotic thoughts of the man giving energy and personality into the seed destined for the egg of the woman, uninterrupted by cogent thought.

There is no law about how to be sexual because the spontaneity of action and desire is the jazz of love danced naked in the flesh, but not completely since the mind controls the sex of man. Only through the power of the man's mind can the sex of man be adjudicated and even then, it is a struggle. No other limb of the body goes to war against the mind. Where the mind rules the body, the penis is a rebel with a mind of his own, expressing himself at inappropriate times without the man's permission. The battle between the mind and the penis reveals the righteous person; to fight one's own nature is to be strong—sex is the smelting pot of desire. The one singular ubiquitous desire pulsing through the blood of man is to know God. Sex is the collusion of the male head and female heart combining as one. The head stands between the soul and the heart; the heart and soul stands between man and God—man is furthest from God requiring help from either the heart of woman or the soul of man. The head is connected to the soul where sex really happens, the male body is just the conduit to woman.

Chapter Six

Woman was made previous to man in a prior world where individuality was championed; in a world where water was predominant and fire was elusive, the two elements combined together producing life by going in—receiving is the nature of all life, in the previous world all energy was focused inward. In this other world, on a different planet, woman came into existence in a most ephemeral way, modestly veiled in the insubstantial mist evaporating beneath the light from the Sun. Man was made from dust gathered from the surface of the Earth, combined with the moisture of woman—kneaded into a physical form with the fingers of light from the stars, blending man and woman into one androgynous body. Woman preceded man by seven thousand years consisting of 974 generations. The emergence of man came at the insistence of woman, because she wanted to have sex. This primal reason for the existence of man validates woman's desire, directing man to serve the desire of woman. When woman is happy, man is happy. When man realizes his place on the Earth is to serve the desire of woman, this will make the next 220 years before entering into the Thousand Years of Woman and Peace, a blissful experience.

Women are likened to the element of water since they are able to meld together as one woman in the same way drops of water meld together to become a pond, a lake, a sea and an ocean. Because of woman's inner energy, they can maintain a balance between being an individual while at the same time blending her vibrations in resonance with other women. Her ability to know is focused in her heart where the connection to the Creator is direct. Knowing translates into love or fear causing the heart to tremble feelings throughout the body to take appropriate actions through the limbs. The knowing of man goes up, uniting with the soul whereas woman goes in, connecting with the Creator. The wheel of life goes from the Creator to the soul to man to woman then back to the Creator, creating movement miraculously achieved in the form of each sin wave contracting through the male zero point, alternating a positive and negative modulation, man and woman equally woven into one movement in the dance of life conducted by the Creator whose wand is directing each vibration in creation into a celestial symphony.

Indeed, the Human Being lives in a two dimensional reality, two sides of the the same human coin, one going in and the other going out; woman naturally wants a house to go into and have a family while man wants to go out to be the provider—sex is the strident example of this primal behavior. The fetus begins as female and all are born from woman, as if a declaration that woman came first. Because woman had a desire for sex, man was then created, which explains many of the discrepancies between the gender. Woman is malleable, able and willing to adjust to the man, whereas the man has one singular objective, to deliver his essence drawn down from the source of his being beyond logic or imagination bursting from his brain channeled through his spine to be cooked in his balls readied to be delivered into the woman with all the force the body can muster. Focused at the lowest point of the triangle into a reservoir of molten fire burning with an insatiable desire for woman whose succulent garden opens to receive the man, sex is the ultimate reward. Woman was made to receive since every impulse within woman goes inward, absorbing the liquid like rain on the ground until muddy, fertile and fecund into a brine of seduction promising a further opening where she can receive man's gift at her innermost.

The male orgasm is opposite from his elemental dust from which man is made; man's orgasm bursts from the heavens then funneled down to the Earth, whereas woman's orgasm percolates from deep within—a coupled orgasm is where the volcano meets the lightening amid a storm of emotions. For man to have a successful orgasm, he needs to hold back until overcome by a force beyond his ability to restrain, while the woman strains to open up and allow the erupting molten energy to lick up the perfume, this sweet gift from the riches gleamed from endless generations coming to culmination at that moment, truly containing multitudes. Though woman comes from the heavens, her orgasm erupts from deep within; while man who is terrestrial has his orgasm originate from beyond, traveling through him as if he is no more than a subservient conduit into woman—man is subservient to woman and at the end of sex man is exhausted and drained, having given everything to his woman. Some men resent this transfer of energy and feel ripped off by the woman but this is obviously the wrong response to sex, rather man should be humbled by woman.

A man who resents a woman after sex does not understand his place in creation nor the importance of love. The translation of אהב/Ahav/Love is, I Give. Giving without reward is greatest type of giving. Sex is filled with endemic reward through every stage. Similarly, in this time, when the six thousand years of man are coming to climax, we find the world is full of fucking and emotional discord with real life ramifications skewing the direction of our world. There are men amongst us who would rather disconnect with woman and instead of giving their essence to the Earth would rather project pointless projectiles into space for no other purpose than quenching their thirst for more, perpetuating the same problems, stuck in the same pointless paradigm. Woman gives man purpose. There is no greater joy to man than to serve woman; there is no nobler cause than the be the source of happiness to our Earth—woman exists on every level and man is conscripted in all his actions to focus for the welfare of women.

The previous world called Tohu/Confusion broke from too much individuality overshadowing the whole. There was huge amounts of light and everything wanted to take in all the light, eventually breaking into 288 (four times seventy-two) sparks conveyed by the burst of water breaking the surface of Mars finding the celestial pathway down to the Earth, which is how Earth came to be full with water and full of life. Earth was seeded from the planet Mars where seven thousand years of incubation led to basic DNA being released upon the Earth. Both Earth and Mars are woman, two types of woman. Mars has a core from ice surrounded by water yet expressing on the surface a harsh burnt exterior gleaming red. Earth is the opposite of Mars, having a pleasant surface of blue oceans, land green with foliage and skies scattered with white clouds, yet having a molten iron core. The fusion from these two women together made man, who would bring the seed of life down from the heavens as a gift and in return she would give him an eternal present from the Earth in the form of a child.

The man is a conduit from Heaven to Earth while woman is the conduit from Earth to Heaven, in that a child represents the continuity of life through the generations. However, before life on Earth could begin, first man had to be tested to see if he had faults. Woman dwelt inside of man, but man could not see the woman. He could only see himself. The Creator took the fire image of this endogenous being into the Garden of Eden. God warned man, do not eat from the tree in the center of the garden. Then God separated the form into gender, male and female. Man, wanting to safeguard his woman, added to the commandment given to him by God. God has said, Not to eat from the tree in the center of the garden but man added, Don't even touch the tree, least you die. God had not forbidden touching the tree but man added this extra precaution so she would keep her distance and not even be tempted. However, his plan backfired when the Serpent came along and pushed her up against the tree and nothing happened. Now the woman had a dilemma. She did not know who to trust. Should she trust the man who had lied to her or should she trust the Serpent her told to eat the fruit.

She ate and then she gave the man to eat. While the man was hiding himself amid the bushes trying to conceal his newly minted foreskin resulting from disobeying God, covering over the first letter in God's Name, י/Yud, the Creator was demanding an answer. Had he eaten from the Tree? The man did not admit to his actions but instead blamed the woman saying, She gave it to me and I ate. The woman then explained how the Serpent had beguiled and tricked her into eating. But, the question was, why did she then give it to the man to eat? She admitted, she did not want to die and the man would marry another. The test had proven, the man to be weak and the woman to be vindictive and therefore they could not remain in the Garden of Eden. Instead, the man and the woman would have to return to the Earth and for six thousand years reclaiming the destruction of clarity by fixing the planet to bring the Garden of Eden down to the Earth. Whereas, the previous world was called, Tohu/Chaos because of the excessive individuality, Earth is called, Tikun/Fixing the inherited misdeeds from our original weak of vindictive parents.

Thirty-five-hundred-years-ago the Written Torah records how a thousand years earlier, long before the flood of Noah, entities were drawn down to the Earth because the women were beautiful. These first five books transcribed by Moshe the Prophet, records how the people were commanded to build a temporary dwelling in the Wilderness called the Mishchan/Dwelling requiring contributions from various materials. The woman attempted to contribute their copper mirrors but Moshe was unsure, since the woman used the mirrors in the vain pursuit of beauty. But, God quickly corrected Moshe the Prophet explaining, The copper mirrors are most important and the most holy since with the mirrors the women made themselves beautiful before their man to entice him to sex. God loves sex because to God, the whole of creation is woman waiting to receive, so God takes on the persona of man, always ready to give. The Creator created creation to be known in low, requiring God to adopt the language of creation to be knowable. Sex is the language of creation: the up and down, the in and out, the alternating current, light undulating between particle and wave and ultimately replicated in the sexual apparatus of man and woman.

Our world is woman, Mother Earth, made beautiful for the purpose of pleasure. She gives herself willingly to man who was given rulership over the land and the sea, over the terrestrial animals, the fish and the birds. Man has dominion over the environment. The attitude adopted by man is reflected throughout the globe. But, man is the dominion of more. As if man no longer loves and instead is using sex as a way to power by transforming his beautiful woman in a whore from which he can make money. What happened to love? Where did love go? Relationships are like two pieces of sandpaper trying to make each other smooth. In the end, man is weak and willing to wipe his hands on the woman; the woman can be vindictive if pushed beyond her limit—love is the litmus between red and blue, between man and woman and between the Creator and the created. Every person on the Earth born of mother carries the obligation to include the Creator in all our activities, so God can better understand the infinite nuances coming from each person fitted with freedom of choice how to interact in God's World. Like children, we invite God into our game of life.

Chapter Seven

The first movement of creation happened when the Creator commanded two lines of light to go and create. The Talmud describes two threads moving along one side of a loom. Not knowing where to go, one thread of light went in and the other thread of light went out; this was the first die of creation, the light going in became male and the light going out became female—a die produces the opposite form. Therefore, in our human forms, woman, who went out goes in, and man who went in, goes out; going out is the focus of Will, while going in is the foundation of Pleasure—the duality of creation goes in and out. Then, there is the up and the down. In terms of light, Heaven is up and Earth is down because there is more light in Heaven than on Earth. Heaven is the intermediary between God who is perfect and all powerful, and the Human Being who is imperfect, weak and broken; the imperfect Human Being mistakenly seeks help from Heaven, not recognizing the channel of effluence is from the Creator—Heaven is almost perfect. The stars in the sky we see as light, are the dark places in Heaven.

Heaven is but a conduit between the Creator and the Human Being on planet Earth where male energy is reflected throughout the globe in man's struggle for domination. The Creator wants to be known in low. There is nothing lower than physicality; men who want gold and dominion are the lowest type person—man has taken hold of power because he is the strongest, able to subjugate others to his Will. Most men, the vast majority of men, have interests other than money and are happy to cede power to those equipped and able. Realistically, we can not truly have dominion over the Earth which belongs to the Melech HaOlam/King of Creation, the Creator; the realization of this basic tenet is key to humility—the arrogant man is the lowest man amid the male gender. Until recently, the protection of woman was the justification for male domination, but in our mostly asexual society this rationale no longer suffices. The intertwining of the genders required for expediency of work plays to the purpose of male domination; men are wearing their pants lower and even shave their pubic hairs—woman has abandoned her beautiful modesty and relinquished her status as woman to be equal to man.

In this time, man exists only for himself, chasing his manifest destiny into outer space. If man's progress were contained to the Earth, eventually the world would become affluent merely from overproduction, but ejaculating our most precious resources into outer space is nothing more than worldwide masturbation into the abyss of nothingness, exacerbating the societal split into rich and poor. Eventually, the poor will be starved to death as the rich require special vetting for every service to servitude. This bleak, self-serving, despotic future seems inevitable given our fear of timelessness, a self-destructive concept of despair, perpetuated by scientific theory; but time is not linear and does not go on forever—time is a spiral segmented into thousand year orbits. Each orbit has a unique color. This thousand year cycle of Yesod/Secret, is when the urgency of the hidden is being awakened and revealed. The thousand years of sex, corresponding to the Sixth Day of Creation when the Human Being was created, has taken hold of the world over the last eight centuries following the Dark Ages, beginning the Renaissance in celebration of the amazing Earth. The greatest light comes out of the darkness, like the light of the eye comes from the black orb of the pupil.

The prior thousand years of darkness, beginning two thousand years ago with the destruction of the Temple in Jerusalem at the hand of Rome, ended a thousand years later with the conclusion of the Dark Ages, with the Black Plague. Rome had decimated the world with their crusades but in the end God incurred upon Rome the scourge of disease to wipe out an equal amount of Romans in a blood for blood exchange. This fifth millennium represented in the time requisite from the Tree of Life is called Hod/Splendor, like the setting sun walking away from the day. In the absence of the light came the darkness when religion took hold in the world by promulgating dogma and ignorance as a way of life. The previous two millennium of Tiferit/Truth and Natzok/Victory, depicted as the torso and the right leg, were eclipsed by the thousand years of Hod, also known as Retreat. During this time of exile of the Jewish People, the Oral Tradition expanded through endless relentless books and manuscripts culminating with the invention of the printing press making knowledge available to everyone. The left leg had stepped back allowing the energy of the body to find the fulcrum in the lower part of the lower triangle, Yesod/Sex.

The Renaissance was the outer manifestation at the beginning of this sexually saturated world, which is now coming to culmination via the premature ejaculation through the aperture of President Donald J. Trump. The afterglow soon faded, followed by something wet and cold, like poverty. The man who promised the world: everything he does or will do, is the best, nothing could be any better; a man oozing with charm, and other things too, has brought male energy to climax—and everyone close to him is getting sprayed by his erratic behavior. But, ejaculations don't just happen, they build up. In each thousand year segment of the six thousand year calendar, the number 666 occurs when sexuality reaches zenith, then over the subsequent 111 years, reaches the 777. In this, the sixth and final day of Creation, the most recent occurrence of the 666 was in 5666/1906; a week prior to the New Year of 5666 which is celebrated in the fall, Einstein published $E=MC^2$ which eventually led to the creation of the atomic bomb. Now, 111 years later, in the year 5777/2017, the cycle of male sex climaxed as the eclipse of 2017, cutting exclusively across the Bible Belt of America, electing Trump as president.

The power of dogma trains the mind to obedience beyond logic. The more foolish the dogma, the greater the faith required to believe. Dogma is a malevolent trick meant to still anxiety and fear, a tree with shallow roots to hold on to in the middle of a storm, a community of weaklings to depend upon. The dogmatic glue locking arms together is endemically false, full of malicious lies like: the Jews kill God, Black People are curse to be slaves, homosexuals are despised by the Creator who created them plus an adamant proclamation, Life begins at conception. This mindless devotion to dogma is fertile ground for a charismatic lowlife able to take control. Mindlessness might be a temporal comfort but the longtime ramifications are staggering. The Roman religion perpetrated on the American People is a hoax, nothing about it is true. The cross is particularly abhorrent because the cross is a symbol of the planet Mars, the place named Tohu/Chaos, to where ancient Rome prays. In 2003 Mars came closest to the Earth, ever. From that time until forever, this was the closest the planet Mars will ever come to the Earth. The power from where Rome suckles life will be in decline, evermore.

History's connection with the stars is not coincidental but rather the well-thought-out plan from the Creator. The division of time into thousand-year segments is immutable, but the story happening within the confines of time is the result of human free will. God is continually writing the Book of Life in Heaven, but the story is dictated through our actions upon the Earth. The long-awaited Thousand Years of Woman and Peace begins in 220 years with the advent of the seventh and final millennium following the six thousand years of man. However, though this exact date is the final demarcation line, there have been numerous signs over the past century, both in the sky and upon the Earth, like the eagle who flits from tree to tree, awakening her young in a manner not to startle. The world has awoken to our common cause of survival not through money and power but through cooperation. This is the final stage of male energy meant to fix this world from the chaos inherited from the previous world of Tohu/Chaos to be repaired by this world called, Tikun/Fixing.

The year 5777/2017 was an important juncture in this process of male energy which, after percolating through thousands of years of human history, achieved this momentous moment for three minutes, the length of the eclipse—the merging point between man and woman. For this sexual metaphor to be understood, it's important to clarify that the production of sperm begins in the brain; the nascent sperm then travels down the spine, is cooked in the balls and is finally delivered to the woman through the vehicle of the penis. The woman's part in coitus requires little more than receiving, which can happen even without her permission, as in rape. Lastly, the sperm quickly dies over a few days, and even the lucky sperm that does fertilize the egg of the woman is quickly absorbed into the egg and subsequently integrated. This process of inception began when first man, barely physical was introduced unto the Earth. Physicality is the wick, but spirit is the flame; however, as time went on, each generation became more physical and therefore less spiritual as the flame retreated back into the ember of the star from where the soul is hewn—over these 5780 years, life has become thickly physical and bereft of light.

The brain is the most ethereal part of the body, connecting to the soul where spiritual worlds exist within the realm of thought. This is where the production of sperm truly begins, in the soul. Incremental thinking can extrapolate from the past into the future, but creative thought can imagine infinity. For a thought to become an actuality, it must first pass through the emotions so expression can be generated. Speech is a type of birth consisting of thoughts, emotions and intentions brought into the physical world through articulated utterances emanating through the subtle vibrating from the lips of the mouth. No animal can replicate this human ability of articulated speech. God spoke and the world began, goes the ancient phrase, but God did not speak words, God broke the Oneness into infinite perturbations reverberating demarcations delineated by differentiations measured in digits. Every separation is bridged by the decimal based on ten: the ten divisions of the human body into three triangles plus the power of speech located in the mouth, the seven continents and three oceans, the Sun and the nine planets, all predicated upon the Tree of Life—ten luminaries upon three vertical pillars: right, left and center.

There are Seven Heavens between Earth and the planet Pluto each with a delineated orbit separating space like continents separated from each other through oceans and stream. However, in Heaven life proliferates in the space in between, not so much on the celestial bodies, which are markers of natural separations. As there is spirituality imbedded within the physical, so too, there are small bits of physicality imbedded within the spiritual. The major distinction shared between Heaven, Earth and Human Being, is the separation between the triangle of the head to the rest of the body. The Sun, Mercury and Venus are distinguished from the other seven celestial bodies by having no moons, a sign life does not inhabit these three orbs but from the Earth on out, life is plentiful. Mother Earth is fecund with physical life, sporting three oceans comprising the brain plus the seven continents the body. Also, in the Human Being there is an obvious distinction between the head housing: thought, sight, hearing, smell and speech, to the rest of the body. The Arctic is the skull, the four lobes of Scandinavia the brain, Eurasia the torso and shoulders, England and Japan the hands, South America and Africa the legs, Canada the back and America the buttocks with the Mississippi River dividing the crack. The Middle East is the female sex and Australia and New Zealand the ovaries.

All celestial bodies came by way of the stars, with the exception of Earth which originated as a pebble at the foot of God's Chair hovering above creation. God wrapped the pebble in various bands of stratum then placed the Earth, called תבל/Tavel with a gematria of 432 in place of the Moon. The harmonic vibrations emanating from the ground has a resonance of 432 hertz. The Earth displaced the Moon at a distance that would perfectly eclipse the Sun by the Moon from the Earth—the Creator's signature. The Human Being is made from 248 limbs and 365 connecting tissues; the Earth circles the Sun every 365 days and Pluto circles the Sun every 248 years—the Tree of Life, replicated throughout creation is key to the ubiquitous Truth apparent in form. The Tree of Life is the fundamental form conducting the workings of creation in both space and time. The six thousand year calendar drawn from the Six Days of Creation conclude with the seventh, the Shabbat, the Day of Rest represented as the Thousand Years of Woman and Peace. The time has come for man to shrug off the white skin of the Serpent, to circumcise the heart so the tongue will only speak the Truth. Man is being called to woman. Who will answer the call? He who will place woman above himself.

Chapter Eight

The difference between love and fucking is in the intention of the action. God judges the Human Being for our intention not our actions; so much can get in the way between the beginning intention and the final action—free choice is not in what we actually do but what we intend to do. There is a natural inclination in man to go inside of woman and there is a nature inclination in woman to want to receive man's gift but the question is why? Both highest and lowest aspects of sex are revelations of Pleasure. On the lower level, the Pleasure of the flesh is paramount but on a higher level, Pleasure is the most ephemeral and delicate experience. The Creator takes great Pleasure in creation yet creation is but a little thing to the Creator. Actually, little and big have no relationship to the Creator but is used in a way of metaphor why God speaks the common sexual language of creation. God's intention in creating creation is to have a dwelling place in low. Time and space are low to the Creator and every aspect to creation is tied to and recognizes the Creator with the exception of the Human Being who needs to chose to be in relationship with the Creator.

Free choice is more than just having rulership over the actions of the body; real free choice is really own found only in the human acceptance or denial to the presence of the Creator in the workings of creation—the true ability of our species is to know the Creator by whatever name, in whatever language. The lower, more physical is the person, the closer the Creator comes to fulfilling the Creator's Desire to be known is low. The thief, before stealing, prays to the Creator for success. Each generation is lower than the previous generation, a concept known as Yeridot HaDorat/Descending Generations; the original light in the space of creation is constantly being attenuated by the ephemeral nature of time—the past quickly erodes while the future is, at best, insubstantial. Only the present persists yet each moment is different, a different opportunity to know the Creator in an even lower environment. The only way to quench God's Thirst is to have true intention to know God in low. When something surprising happens, the Human Being can attribute the happening to God or to nature; some say God and nature are the same but this is not true—God is the Creator of nature through means of the name Elohim/God of Plurality with the gematria of 86 the same gematria as the word Hateva/The Nature.

Nature is regulated by instinct. Each living creation or plant or even stone has a particular nature continually transmitted to their offspring; the gold nugget breaks down into gold dust, the plants produce seeds and animals produce replicas with instinctual progeny—only the human being is free to direct our intention to our actions. Though most human actions rely on social or institutionalized behavior to conduct ourselves through the world, nonetheless, the intention of the action, no matter what the action entails, can be a deliberate attempt to satisfy the longing of the Creator. The Creator is tied to every created physical form or spiritual entity governed by a nature able to be parted at any time to perform a miracle, a happenstance beyond nature, defying what is expected. Freedom of choice is what evokes miracles; not to be complacent and accept what is offered—but rather to change the course of history through the power of intention. As easily as one can fuck, one also gets fucked, depending on the intention of each participant. The constant question needing a constant answer is, what is the intention? What is being given? Is it love or fuck, that is the question?

If the intention is pure, intending to bring the Creator closer to creation, then the action of sex has no rules, no restrictions and is beautified by the Creator. There is no more profound act than sex, an action caused by time and space melding into one through the combined intentions of man, woman and God. Similarly, countries and nations through their adherence to a constitution or an ancient tradition, affix the intention of the people towards the future. These fortresses of human spirit causes the cohesion of nations to gather together with a common understanding. However, when the intention becomes skewed then the true path is lost and chaos ensues. The people feel they are getting fucked but it is hard to prove motive. Dynasties are dangerous because intention becomes institutionalized; religion is the most dangerous of all since they govern through dogma—when the intention fails or is subverted, the people lean into the dogma for strength and clarity. However, no dogma or institutionalized way of thinking can make up for intention, rather dogma is an expedient way to subvert the Truth in favor of a hidden agenda, setting the stage for the rape of the nation.

This curious word, Fuck, does not describe a bodily function like most crude indecent words, but rather a hidden scheme, like a man being nice to a woman only for the sake of sex. Women are easily convinced; the seduction from a man is often a process of taking advantage of vulnerabilities particular to women—the sound of the voice, the words spoken. A woman can want to have prurient sex as much as she desires, but for most woman their sexual energy is directly tied to their heart, which requires a man winning the heart of a woman first before going for the sex. Seduction is winning the heart of woman with an illegitimate foray of lies and intentional deceptions. Fucking is a type of stealing whereas sex is an open compact made in an unfettered transaction. No relationship can stand up to the lie of a false heart or a scheming mind. Fuck is a ubiquitous term known throughout the world without the necessity of translation because we all know about getting fucked. Once fucked, the question is how to get unfucked? How to revive trust after being fucked is tricky business often consisting of political theater full of further lies.

Do we reconcile or do we divorce, now that is the question? The same question left to couples is just as relevant to a society needing to move beyond the past. The only reason for marriage is sex, because all other activities can be done irregardless; commitment of marriage makes the sex better, which is the reason for marriage—patriotism is the commitment to one's country binding the citizens together. But, love is a fickle emotion, easily supplanted. When love is gone, what then? America has become is nation of expedient practicality, living together in a constant quibbling over every aspect and circumstance, not allowing life to happen, instead manipulating every action to a hidden agenda to a false and brazen god by means of misinformation, or in other terms, lying. Once distrust enters into a relationship, the relationship is over, whatever remains is a relationship of convenience until it becomes inconvenient and the relationship is finally over. There are three types of sex: everywhere sex when the relationship first begins, then bedroom sex as the relationship moderates and finally hallway sex, when they meet in the hallway and say, Fuck you—meaning, the relationship is over.

The word Fuck is a universal word having the same meaning in every language; sixty years ago when I was in high school they called it, The Word—no one actually vocalized The Word because it was the ultimate conversation stopper. Even now, Fuck is termed the F-Bomb when spontaneously said while receiving a reward. Vice President Biden leaned over President Obama's shoulder to say just prior the signing the Healthcare Bill into law, "This is big fucking deal." The word Fuck is so bad and so ubiquitous throughout the world, it can be employed in good or bad situation or in describing beauty or excellence as in, Being fucking great. So what goes with the word Fuck? The word Fuck originated centuries ago when the King of England wanted to divorce his wife, but the Holy Roman Catholic Church disallowed divorce, so the king created a new religion, the Church of England where divorce was allowed. Previous to the Church of England, if the king wanted a new queen he simply cut off the head of the old queen before remarrying. The people took some time to get use to the new standard, seeing the king prance around with a new queen while the old queen was still alive.

Soon the people began imitating the king by characterizing their own tryst as, Fornication Under Consent of the King, which was a mouthful to say, so eventually shorten into the acrostic, Fuck. The king is the highest authority in the land and all must obey his wishes and commands, even if he is being a hypocrite or a liar, the people, his subjects, are bound by their love and devotion to the king. The word Fuck breaks the bond between the king and people leaving only a shell of the previous relationship for the sake of convenience. Religion through their dogma are practicing the art of Fuck. Yet, even religion has a way of slowly self-correcting through the kind people from the southern hemispheres forced into the servitude of religion, find ways to soften the blow, like taking Jesus down from the cross and replacing old stale Latin liturgy with gospel music. The intrepid nature of life wars with dogma and platitudes until vanquished by the truth. Fuck is the casting off of restraints, good or bad; Fuck is the final, exasperated attempt at communication before thrusting the sword into the heart of whatever was being said, the ultimate exclamation point—Fuck is a four-letter bomb.

Not incidentally, God's Name YHVH is also four letters, a word the Jewish People are not allowed to say, plus the tradition of the pronunciation has been lost. The Creator balanced creation between good and bad, male and female, night and day; the balance to the word Fuck is the YHVH from whose four letters can be interchanged to make four Hebrew words: היה/Hoya/Past; הוה/Hova/Present and יהיה/Yehiye/Future. Bodily functions are dirty and often used to describe our world and the people with whom we share this planet, but the word Fuck describes when the human being becomes a demon and suddenly you know you are fucked because demons have no compassion, at all. The spiritual manifestation making man into a concept is found in the Kesay HaCovid/Holy Chariot, a metaphoric image of a chair being held up by three animals: Shor/Ox, Areya/Lion and Nesher/Eagle. Upon the chair is the image of a man going higher and higher being continually lifted by the three animals. From the sweat of the three animals combine to make the boiling raging waters forming the River Denar where the soul immersing to forget physical sensation. The three animals lifting the chair upon where sits the man, is a metaphoric lesson to each human being.

The three animals correspond to the three segments of the human body. Each person is required to train their animal, beginning with training the body to withhold excrement until the appropriate time and place. We continue throughout life training our mind, emotions plus our words and actions not to inflict pain upon the world in our attempt at perfection. We admire people who are perfect in any endeavor because physical life is so imperfect. The man is higher than the animals as a sign, the man has free choice and the ability to rule the animal. The Chair in the metaphor is the place where God sits judging man. Obviously, God has no body or image because God is the Creator of creation and in no way can be described or defined using the elements of creation. Nonetheless, since the Creator wants to be known in low, God had to adopt creation's multitude of expressions to be used in metaphor. A chair brings the body closer to the Earth. By God coming down closer to the Earth, the physical world combined with the human spirit residing within the animal body comes closer to the Creator. Reality is a collusion of the animal, the human and the Creator as depicted in the Kesay HaCovid.

Chapter Nine

The ancient name our of planet is, Tavel, with a gematria of 432 which is the resonant vibration of the Earth. Until 1950, musicians tuned their instruments to 432 hertz, then the necessity to collaborate with technology musicians were forced to adopt a new standard, 440 hertz. Also, the word Tavel in Hebrew depicts a person having sex with an animal, therefore the name of our planet is Tavel, a place where the human soul and animal body merge. Much of the consternation in life arises from the discord attributed to the collusion of animal and human into one body, each having different goals. The animal goes on all fours, constantly looking down at the ground while the human being goes erect looking up into the heavens, dreaming about what could be, unimpeded by instinct. The Human Being can hit a target with a rock, an arrow or spaceship because we have the uncanny ability extrapolate into the future while the rest of creation lives in the present, controlled by their individual instincts. The Human Being, particularly men, have rulership over our planet and the responsibility to guard the environment and to do right to others, beginning with our women and our children.

The importance of understanding true reality is epitomized by the way our world came into being, the fulcrum from where all extrapolations begin, where all futures have their genesis and where a fundamental cognitive mistake has grown into a huge obstacle, obscuring and blocking world-wide enlightenment and peace. This fundamental mistake is embedded in scientific fact concerning time and space. The universe, according to science, goes on forever dragging time into infinity; a dystopian future full of purposelessness—atrophying into the endless vacuous nothing. Our puny attempts at establishing monuments, anchoring ideas to the ground in a feeble effort to overcome the inevitable disintegration of matter is nothing more than the withering male ego. Calendars are equally divisive, an arrogant attempt to establish meaningless demarcations into oceanic time in a futile endeavor at demarcation. However, The Big Bang Theory is unsubstantiated, only proven through wild assumption then taught to children and their parents as if they were facts; yet, the Human Being who was created along with the rest of creation, intuits the opposite must be true—instead of something coming out of nothing, which is just plain illogical, nothing must have come out of something. Truth is found in the framework of creation, patterned by the Creator and pervasive throughout the universe.

Since God is the author of this story, time is short, attached to limited space as instituted by the Creator at the beginning of creation. Once started, creation was intent on continuing to the infinite future until God shouted at creation to stop. Using the command, די/Di/Enough, God became called by the Name שדי/Shadi/Said Enough with a gematria of 314, the first three numbers in pi, the mathematical construct weaving the line and the curve into one. Time is a function of space and therefore is equally constrained. Constraint leads to form engraved out of the OreAinSof/LightWithoutEnd spitting out shards of incoherence, creating and destroying until the Creator was satisfied with the configuration. After 266,450,000 years began the Six Days of Creation prototype to the subsequent six thousand male years of creation (the present date is 5780) before entering into the Thousand Years of Woman and Peace corresponding the seventh day of the week, the Shabbat/Day of Rest. The lower seven components of the Tree of Life are replicated in the Six Days of Creation and the seventh day, the Shabbat/Day of Rest. The lower two triangles found in the Tree of Life represent man infused with the female during six thousand years ultimately merging with woman in 220 years.

These last 780 years have been an expression of sexuality replete with upheavals in creativity and in war, eight centuries of tumultuous human behavior culminating in our time as the 666 collides with the 777. In historical terms, the movements of man upon the Earth over six millennium has brought the entirety of the world to one point. In the same way the ultimate goal of sexual energy is to bring forth the essence of the human spirit drawn out of the soul into the head imbued with the totality of human gnome drawn down the spine of time. The cooking of the sperm in the two testicles is representative of the last two thousand years of Roman exile; the world inoculated into Roman ways awaiting the final redemption—the ejaculation. The thoughts and intentions within the mind of man during ejaculation is transferred to woman, a garment in which the pregnancy is encapsulated. Men should not have sex while drunk or angry for fear this energy might be transmuted in birth. With every sexual intercourse there is conception and birth in Heaven which is natural, but on Earth birth is a miracle.

Every aspect of sex, conception and birth is constantly happening in Heaven mimicking the sexual interchange between the genders, driven by corporeal exploits on Earth. The terrestrial land is woman; Heaven rains down upon woman through the vehicle of man—the continuity of our species is seen in each new generation. However, this time 2020, represents a radical change, a deliverance from the servitude of compelled actions into the freedom of ultimate expression from the soul down to the head of the penis where the first letter י/Yud in the name in YHVH is engraved into the flesh of each man. A recognition to our purpose in the world, to protect, impregnate and care for woman and her children is commiserate with caring for the Earth. During the time of ejaculation, everything pales in the face of the ejaculate and the accompanying energy like an arrow being driven by a powerful bow. Male masturbation weakens the strength of the bow, robbing the woman of her essential reward. Sex is a transaction where man is expected to have a good product to deliver, on time and according to the needs of the woman.

These six thousand years of male history, where woman is reduced to a helpmate, are coming to climax; we can all feel the culmination coming, for five decades since the end of the Sixties—but, suddenly the man is impotent, unable to produce anything of value other than his own ego. The bastion of Roman religion, Roman war, coin of Rome, industry of Rome and the unrelenting obsession with world domination is America. What is happening in the world, is the final fall of Rome when, The wolf will finally lie down with the lamb; and the lion with eat straw with the ox—the prophesy for the End of Days written three thousand years earlier. Both the Hebrew and Mayan calendars are immutable since they are based on naturally occurring cycles, 26,000 years in the Mayan calendar coalescing with the seven thousand year human history of man on Earth as reflected in the six thousand year calendar adopted by the Jewish People. The Torah/Teaching of the Jewish People, is primarily concerned with establishing a timeline from the very beginning then meticulously accounting for each subsequent generation.

Woman preceded man by seven thousand years, being developed in Tohu/Chaos where mental agility swam in the waters hidden beneath the harsh ruddy surface. Each generation in Tohu was seven years long, a subtle current passing through the continually changing ether eventually producing lifeforms vacillating between potential and real, like a porpoise momentarily dancing upon the surface of the water. Tohu, the previous world was triangulated, arising from a point expressed in three elements: fire, air and water, easily fitted together in an ephemeral transitory form transmitted through the heavens from the Creator. Each of the lower seven attributes on the Tree of Life wanted to receive, to encompass and to contain all the light, causing each to break following a seven year pattern, like the seven musical notes. After seven thousand years, the entire world broke is a gush of galactic water rushing in torrents through the pathways in the heavens until reaching the Earth, inundating the land with oceans covering the ground, planting each form from the previous world into the succulent Earth to arise and take on life with the added element of Earth. Woman's demand for sex was met with the creation of אדם/Adom/Man whose three letters can be interchanged to make the word מאד/Moed/More.

There is an ancient Hebrew saying, the womb of woman can never be satisfied. These six thousand years of man at the behest of woman have come to a conclusion, the gathering energies throughout the planetary bodies including all life forms funneled down to the place of sex ready to deliver the payload to satisfy woman's wants but suddenly the man has gone impotent because he is not a real man and has nothing essential to give. Suddenly the woman feels she is being fucked, used for his pleasure without giving her anything; what is his, belongs to him and what is her's, also belongs to him—the basic definition of, getting fucked. Our world, the ultimate expression of woman, is sick of getting fucked by rich people who only want to use her, who have no respect for woman, no empathy for pain and no intention to love. The false man disguises his true intentions with a flamboyant personality, promising anything, appealing to the lowest instincts of weak men by attacking woman and wiping his hands on her. The Earth is sick and prayed to the Creator who sent Covid to the world, a word Covid in Hebrew which means, Respect.

Men are forever blaming women for their inadequacy; men take out their rage with their hard fists against the soft flesh of woman, where is housed a delicate feminine soul—a man who attacks a woman is a monster. Nothing can substitute for virility, not a big dick, handsome face or well sculpted body. There is another ancient saying, There is no erection without the inclusion of the third eye, the seat of Knowing from where the body connects to the crown of the soul ushering in new life. Virility is the inner energy fueled by good intention spoken in an unspeakable soft voice full of love. Love in Hebrew is אהב/Ahev; Hev means Give and the letter Aleph in the beginning indicates—I. The "I" of the person is harbored deep inside the consciousness; the purest expression of the person—the woman inside of each man.

Men who block and disregard the woman within, does so for himself and his own self-adoration. Men are generally bigger than woman as to give each man a choice as to how he will treat his woman; he can overpower her or he could disregard his strength and bow to her wishes—this is freedom of choice.

The trials and tribulations faced by both genders and all the in between varieties harbored within these two extremes of man and woman, are played out on this physical plane of existence and replicated throughout societies everywhere in the world. America is a country comprised of people from throughout the globe. America is like a little world. What happens in America has tremendous reverberations throughout the globe, just take the Sixties. How America responds at this juncture in world history when the 666 is trying to break through the 777 will inevitably be a turning point defining man for the next thousand years, the Thousand Years of Woman and Peace. By shrugging off the glistening white snakeskin posing as capitalism, to instead fixate our attention on the welfare women, children and Earth we can quickly redeem of world and all the men of the world. What will happen in the remaining 220 years can liberate the world and all the conflicts can be settled because the world is wired. Another ancient prediction is, In the End of Days what is done is one place in the Earth will immediately be heard throughout the world. We are coming alive in one body and she is woman.

Chapter Ten

The ascension of woman began fifty years ago in 1970 which was 5730 in the Hebrew calendar which is the half-life of carbon-14, a significant fact considering the metaphor of the king saying to his queen, I will give to you half of my kingdom. The Sixties flamed out under the auspices of Richard Nixon whose election in 1968 was heralded in by the LA Free Press with the headline: Dick In. After six millennium, finally woman has awoken and is getting aroused. Coined, Female Waters by Jewish mystics, the idea of woman rising up from depth within her core where exploding volcanic eruptions burst into streams of pleasure, has quietly permeated the world to the extent men are shaving their pubic hair and wearing their pants lower on their hips. Our world was made by the Creator for Pleasure as indicated by the two natural occurring crops, one in Afghanistan where poppies grow a medicine able to block pain, and the other in Columbia where the Coco plant gives energy for those in famine. Between famine and pain, life is lived in Pleasure since Pleasure is the essential element in life.

Another ancient saying, All sevens are beloved. Woman is the seventh component of the Seven Medot/Measurements stemming from the Ten Sefirot/Luminaries grown upon the Tree of Life. Seven is conclusion and rest, as in the Day of Rest on the seventh day of the week. From this rest, the new week is blessed by the power of seven as portrayed by four prayer sessions in which seven blessing are silently intoned; the night prayer, the morning prayer and the added prayer around noon, makes 777. Thus the end of the previous week followed by the final afternoon prayer of seven blessings beginning the new week. Everything revolves around the seven because woman is seven and because woman wanted sex, man was created and now that we only 220 years before the Thousand Years of Woman and Peace, she has become predominate. After fifty years of woman ascension, the worldwide paradigm shift is happening, empowering woman. This cosmic shift is directed by the response from man. The time of excess and obsession has reach an end, the dominion of man has ended, he must step aside to be part of the future, he must hold woman above himself, so woman can crown man.

One of the ancient predictions concerning our time, the End of Days the end of the male calendar is, Laws managing the Land of Israel will be extended throughout the world; every seven years the land must rest—after seven cycles, the fiftieth year called Jubilee is forever. Woman has been ascending for fifty years since 1970, and has reach the permanence of forever. Now, the time has come for man to meet woman's challenge by bringing forth the true man who has been shackled and manipulated, enslaved by false values, skewed facts and outright lies. Now, is the time to bring forth man's essence, the perfume satiating woman's pleasure, the sweet elixir feeding her soul. Woman has suffered beneath man's rulership but now the torch is being handed to woman so she can rule, bringing rest to man. Ending is the most beautiful part of work, being able to rest after a job well done. No matter the past, if an endeavor ends well then redemption is found in the future, what went before is obliterated in the celebration.

Originally, God created the human being an androgynous person able to conceive and birth offspring, but because man was unable to see woman, God split them into two equal and opposite genders. Man goes out, woman goes in. The time has begun for the sexes to reunite. Another ancient prophesy is, At the end of the Thousand Years of Woman and Peace, the human soul will become one, then travel to another world (Mars was the first world, Earth the second world so logically one might suspect the future world will be on Jupiter or one of the many moons) for another seven thousand year cycle eventually bringing alive the seven outer planets over 49,000 years until the Sun, Mercury and Venus become conscious. At birth, sustenance ends in the stomach and begins from the head. Man is the lowest form of creation and by that virtue can lift the entirety of creation like a lever placed at the lowest point to lift the entirety. Woman is man's motivation. The time has come to tear off the facade and be real. The Sixties planted the seed and by the Seventies various endeavors were taking hold: computers, war, politics, religion, economy and space exploration.

After fifty years, all man has to offer is more. More of the same old. The time has come to cast off the whit Skin of the Serpent preventing the real expression of man. Man needs to hold woman above himself so woman can crown man. The Covid virus has come to America to free man from the burden of working for other men, when we should be working for woman and the interests of woman. The simple secret is, When woman is happy then man is happy. There is no panic because there is nowhere to run. There is time to sit and think, contemplate the meaning of life. Here in the center of creation, here upon the Earth where man reigns supreme thrusting forth his freewill wherever he pleases according to his free choice is now being tested, the final test to see if man has become strong and no longer wipes his hands on his woman but instead puts her before himself in every expression of woman from the Earth to the womb and back again. The meticulous workings of the world including the sectioning of time is how the Creator speaks loud and clear, if anyone is interested in listening. Or maybe not?

Freedom of choice has nothing to do with our mundane decisions made throughout life because much in life is predictable; the real choice is moment to moment, available at every moment, answering the ancient question—where is God? Modern knowledge says, When there is a fork in the road, take it. The road of life forks from the very beginning and continues forking forever. One path leads toward God because God is everywhere; the other path leads into chaos, where freedom is confined to the human experience. This choice is always before us, as each moment ticks away challenging the person to make a choice. God wants to be known in low, each moment is lower than the previous moment, closer to the final culmination concluding and fulfilling God's Desire to be known in low. Because of the time restraints put on creation from the very beginning, time is running out. After six millennium, with only 220 years remaining before man completely merges into women, what will satisfy the Creator's Desire to be known in low? What can be done, which has not yet been done? Should we be looking to outer space?

Another ancient saying, God spoke and the world came into existence. God did not speak words, God spoke value, differentiation achieved by breaking the One Light into subtle reverberation through time and space. God speaks to the world in many ways, the most meticulous is by means of numbers. The Six Days of Creation and the Seventh Day of Rest is the primordial beginning of the male-female paradigm, reflected in the twelve zodiacal divisions of the sky through which the Earth moves counting the six months from fall to spring as male, and from spring to fall as female. Implicit in each twelve is the thirteen. אחד/Echud/One has a gematria of thirteen. All creation lives within the sacred geometry of creation; each life, like a drop of water slowly moving to the sea, navigates through the ground, seeking the ocean—all ways lead to God, if the rudder of intention is set in that direction. Sex is the most integrative genuine human activity, guided from Heaven, infused with God's presence, sex is the ultimate metaphor to every aspect of life. Sex has an end, a culmination where the long awaited climax needs to deliver essence.

The energy of the world has been revved up through an extraordinary effort put forth by technology, assembled by people around the world and paid for by consumption of worthless, meaningless products meant to turn the unsuspected stupid, then ignorant and finally imbecilic. Progress is constantly stirring up a vapid environment producing a new reality for the coming generation. A self perpetuating plan meant to subvert the path with a heart imbedded in the Tree of Life into a path proclaiming life, an incidental occurrence, a temporal happening within the chaos of nihilism. God speaks in the text of the Torah saying, I put before you good and bad, chose good. The choice is in each person to consciously invite the Creator into your life, converse with the Creator who is everywhere all the time to everybody. Because God is not of creation and because all of creation is like one person to the Creator, the necessity of each person to consciously intercourse with the Creator helps God be known in low. The Creator can not really know creation but through the human beings who possess freedom of choice, where Truth is one choice and illusion is another choice.

There is a point in sex, just before ejaculation happens, when both the man and woman halt movement, the woman waiting to receive while the man eminently expecting a rush of essence through his impaled body, pinned and fastened into the final thrust forward. This event has just happened upon the Earth, which was moving faster and faster then suddenly stopped. The entire body of the Earth became still with anticipation. We think we are waiting for the virus to subside but this is not the Truth. The virus was send to us from God to bring about this moment in time when the calendar had reached 5,780 years. Eighty in Hebrew is represented the letter פ/Peh/Mouth. The mouth is the place in the body depicting woman. The three triangles of the body composed of male and female energies; the left and right combine in the middle are ultimately expressed through the lips of the mouth—woman. After fifty years of woman ascension, the time has come to make a stand and prepare to receive an essential illumination from the Creator leading us to the finish line. Each generation is the repository of the entirety of the human endeavor, good and bad.

There is a plea for unity happening throughout the world, an antiracist acknowledgement that all people are truly created equal. The blend of human beings is beautiful and the only bad element in a person is found in his actions; yet, God does not judge a person's soul on the actions of their body but rather on the intentions in the heart. As the phony construct made from philosophical arrogance crumbles beneath the weight of Truth, something new and beautiful is about to happen, then expand during 220 years towards the advent of the

Thousand Years of Woman and Peace. Everything has stopped awaiting the world to fix our communal attention to the needs of the Earth, the children of the Earth and the mothers who care for them. Women needs and deserves to be put back up upon the pedestal of respect. Love is flowering in the world, a gentle love that children understand. What is holding back the love we all want so desperately? Why are we arguing over politics while our people are suffering? Who is actually running this show and for what purpose? There is an opposition and that opposition is, the disease of arrogance.

PART TWO
Chapter One

Religion separates the sexes, imposing unfounded impositions between man and woman in a profoundly personal way resulting in Pirud/Separation. The foundation of the previous world Tohu/Confusion was caused from an overabundance of individuality causing separation. Sex, one of the Eser Sefirot/Ten Illuminations, was left dormant until woman decided she wanted to have sex. Indeed, according to Jewish Law, the man is forbidden to have sex with his wife until she wants to have sex. Man is meant to be in service to woman and as a result, if woman is happy then man is happy. Religion reviles woman as the causation of sin, the temptress using her flesh and smile to divert man from his righteous path. Having just become a nation and received the Torah, the Jewish People were commanded to build the Mishkan/Tabernacle in the Wilderness according to the donations given by the people. The women gave their copper mirrors but Moshe was unsure to receive them since the women used their mirrors in the pursuit of vanity. God answered, These are the most holy of all since through the mirrors the women sexually excited the men, bringing forth the Jewish People.

    The imposition of religion, particularly when it comes to sexual matters, has caused the four letter word, Love, to be replaced by the four letter word, Fuck. Interesting how the Church preaches love but then in the shadow of their institution, they fuck. Fornication Under Consent of the King is a real thing. Religion has crowned themselves king, decreeing made-up law based on baseless stories and prejudice. Through religion, Rome was able to institute what the sword had been unable to accomplish. The Empire of Rome never fell, they just transformed into the Holy Roman Catholic Church replete with their absurd story about how the Jews killed god, how Black People are cursed to be slaves forever, and how God hates homosexuals, plus papal proclamation, Life begins at conception. Yet, beyond it all, the slandering of woman is the worst; placing woman beneath man to serve his desire is in complete opposition to how the world works—an indecent attempt to rest woman from the arms of God and place her beneath the weight of man, when the opposite is true. Man is a conduit between Heaven and Earth; man is furthest from the Creator—man needs to hold woman above himself, in order to reconstruct our world.

Upon leaving Egypt 3500 years ago, the nascent Jewish nation was attacked by the ancient people known as Amaleke. God considered this assault against this infant nation as pedophilia and vowed the Name YHVH would not be whole until Amaleke is forever destroyed. Finding the genitals of the dead torn off and thrown skyward at the end of battle is a sign of Amaleke as if to say, They sinned in their sex and deserved to die. The Church makes the same declaration saying, All children are born into sin; masturbation is the cause of eternal damnation and women are innately evil. Religion is a cauldron of boiling blood overflowing with every evil of the world, then absolving sin in a wafer. The Church, the father of all religion, since there is no word for religion in Hebrew, Arabic or Sanskrit, has brazenly replaced God in the triangle of life where the Creator makes union holy by being one of the participants in sex. By creating both the man and woman, moment by moment, God is able to experience life moment by moment through creation. Religion has wrecked sex and by doing so has inflicted the world with Fuck. Fuck is everywhere, Fornication Under Consent of the King—just do what they do.

Fuck lives in the lie. The Jewish People were the first to get fucked by the Church who took Jesus, a Jewish Rabbi prophet and impaled him on the cross for two thousand years. The cross is a symbol of the previous world Tohu/Chaos; Jesus was put on the cross by the Romans according to their story but blamed on the Jews who did not intercede. A simple way to know this story never happened is there is no historical evidence even of Jesus ever living, none. Only through the Koran, which like the Torah, is prophecy coming from the same Heaven reverberating the wishes of the Creator, do we know the Truth. In the Koran, Jesus is considered a prophet. The Koran explains, the Rabbis from that time could not accept the sign of Jesus' virgin birth and thus the last prophet would not be Jewish but Arab, Mohammad the Prophet. But there is nothing about the biblical cross, just a made-up hateful story decimating the Jewish population over two thousand years. The Jewish and Arab Peoples are the sum total of the Semitic race. Our languages come from Avraham who had lived in the Tower of Babel and knew the secret to language. Avraham knew the twenty-two movements of the mouth and thus was able to derive the first two phonetic languages, Arab and Hebrew, able to record exact speech.

The languages of the world were fit together from the shards fallen to the Earth after the destruction of the One Language used to build the Tower of Babel. Arabic and Hebrew, fashioned by Avraham, are whole languages able to receive prophecy. The Bible is a made-up story trying to piece together an illogical theory with no corroboration. Plus, the Church had the audacity to change the translation of the Torah/Teaching into Testament. The difference between these two names is, Teaching welcomes questions whereas Testament despises questions because the dogma is beyond being questioned. Religion's intrusion into the arena of sex has muddied the pure sacred water of an essential human activity, where according to God's Law all sexual desires are permitted. Rome's obsession with conquering the world is only satisfied when they are fucking someone. Rome's final victory over the Jews, swallowing the sword, humbled upon her knees, the Jewish woman Monica Lewinsky and President Clinton in the Oval Office of the White House. Sex is implicit in politics where leader are elected who love their country and the people but once in power, love turns to Fuck. The word Fuck needs to be freed, since it is the only word in worldwide lexicon of words that adequately addresses our worldwide predicament.

Money is the cum of fucking, politics is their tool fucking with their Crossite religion. The ancient sign of Mars, where individuality led to chaos and destruction, is the cross. Money and politics go together, the two sexual partners; religion is the substitute for God—hiding in the shadows, murmuring incantations. Of all the idols from ancient times, Bal Peor was the worst and for that reason Moshe was buried opposite this idol as if to say, these are the best and the worst of this world. A person cannot be better or be closer to God than Moshe who had the Keys to the Palace; and no one can be worse than Bal Peor, also known as the Shitgod—people had such fear from this idol they would lose control of their bowls while visiting the site. Eventually, as the fear subsided, shitting in front of this idol became the custom. The sacrifice to Bal Peor was accomplished by bringing a child to pass through the fire of pedophilia. The first nation to attack the Jewish People was Amaleke who was also famous for sexually abusing children. Abusing children is bad but abusing children sexually is horrible.

One of the Seven Commandments given at the advent of man and woman, therefore applicable to all peoples, is to make laws relevant to sexuality for the purpose of protecting woman and children. Sexuality is the core of our being and each person should be allowed to explore this undefined and undefinable aspect of life without interference from external morals. Unfortunately, in this time when pornography is thrust before a child's eyes at an earlier and earlier age, childhood is quickly lost, abandoned to confusion. This is the last thousand year period, dedicated to sexuality through the lower point of the triangle comprising the Tree of Life, called Yesod/Foundation taken from the word Sod/Secret. All secrets are being revealed at this time, 220 years before the end of this last millennium before the advent of the Thousand Years of Woman and Peace. Both the good and the bad are being revealed but mostly the truth is being revealed. Two thousand years ago, the Zohar was written down by Shimmon ben Yechoi in a space between Heaven and Earth, with the admonition, these words are meant for the End of Days, end of the six thousand year male agenda.

The Zohar was transmitted to the Earth a thousand years later, to a mystic in Spain named Moshe DeLeon who wrote down the text then died. Eventually this hefty volume was bought by a rich man who understood the profundity of the words. Later, the Zohar was put into print. For hundreds of years no one could understand the words of the Zohar until five hundred years ago when the Ari came to Northern Israel to illuminate the world with the Cabala, a secretive knowledge passing through the soil until erupting into a spring where the illuminated could connect with the hidden knowledge. A couple of hundred years later, the spring began streaming into Europe where the Chasidim fed this knowledge to the simple people—that was ten generation ago. The Truth is bursting upon the scene; those in the government who have watched us are now being watched by us—the mirror has become a window and the shade is being lifted. This is why the Zohar, an obscure text written in ancient Hebrew and Aramaic, written two thousand years ago is meant for our time when this knowledge can be readily deciphered by those able to look into the heavens. What science has discovers, corroborates what was described in the Zohar, two thousand years ago.

The Zohar is a meticulous rendering of creation from the original black hole down to our Earth, embedded in our solar system. Described as a small space within a large space, intertwining the solar system within our Milky Way Galaxy, the Zohar clearly depicts the outer seven celestial bodies in our solar system. There are lengthy texts within the Zohar tracing the perturbations between endless worlds to produce sustenance on this physical plane transmuted with life drawn from the stars. Four thousand years ago, Avraham writes in the Sefer Yitzira/Book of Formation referring to the celestial bodies, There are ten and not nine; there are ten and not eleven. Science can detect a large planetary body beyond the Kuiper Belt where Pluto is enmeshed at the edge of the solar system, but cannot pinpoint the place until speculating, perhaps it is a sort of black hole that does not reflect light. The Zohar explains, This place is the Garden of Eden, the side facing the universe, is full of ethereal light; while the side facing the solar system is the mouth of Moma who swallows all souls to purify spirit and clarify memory—Gehinnom. The Zohar describes this place, being large as the planet Saturn with the rings included. The Zohar illuminates creation so science can corroborate, The universe is designed, created and sustained by the Creator.

The ramifications of this inevitable corroboration between factual scientific discovery and ancient knowledge acknowledging the innate design of creation will eliminate any doubt. Life did not just spontaneously happen. Life was planned from the beginning by the Creator who continues to create moment by moment without the necessity of religion, at all. Religion is not respected in Heaven because religion sells Heaven for money and power, a thing that has destroyed America, the bastion of freedom. The Native Americans where right, the land of America cannot be bought or sold. The American Constitution based on the Iroquois Confederacy is a marriage contract with the people who populate this country, both citizens and non-citizens. The Federal Government has become over the last five decades, an abusive husband. And now while the American people are suffering, the leader, the President and his enablers have shown no empathy for the people. The only solution is divorce. By divorcing the Federal Government, we the People can reclaim the land and the housing to house the people so society can function as a whole. Better to be a single mother than to be abused by a heartless husband.

Chapter Two

The Zohar teaches, Adom Kadmin/Primodial Form is perfect in all directions from the highest point plus the sides, but the direction down is imperfect; therefore, there is a general energy coming up from below in our effort to become perfect before God—yet, man is full of inherent imperfection. Because this world is in a constant state of disintegration, perfection can only be momentary. The first dot of creation expanding downward naturally took on imperfection. From thinker to athlete, from painter to builder, from man to woman, each has a sense of possible perfection driving the person to do better. The performance of perfection is what draws the crowd. When perfection is accomplished, in any fashion or expertise, the ramifications reverberate back to this pre-spiritual first form, changing everything throughout creation from the highest place. For Adom Kadmin to come closer to the Creator, is in opposition to God's Desire to be known in low, the imperfect. Two opposite threads are from the very beginning of creation, one going up and in towards God while other is going down into low, into time and space where each imperfect Human Being is the star of the story.

After 5,780 years, man has become completely physical, the lowest human beings ever to live on this planet, as evidenced by the global obsession with money—the most corporeal element of all physicality, plus our obsession with gadgets meant to protect us from nature. Only the gross form of physicality dwelling on the Earth amid constant divisions, crumbling into dust, generation after generation can satisfy the longing of the Creator to be known in low. In the Earth's seven continents, America is the buttocks, the lowest place in the human form, able to sit upon the ground. The United States of America has become the Divided States of America. More than any other nation in the world, America espouses the Roman paradigm in the six heads of Rome: coin, religion, war, technology, institutions and politics. Rome, whose spiritual source is drawn from the previous world Tohu/Chaos in the planet Mars famous for independence, is the lowest energy on the Earth. When a wall falls, the top bricks fall the furthest. As witnessed by their brutality in all of their six avenues of expression, Rome has found his home in America. The Black and Brown Peoples forced to accept Roman ways have softened Rome by bringing southern kindness into northern severity.

By the year two thousand in the Roman calendar, Rome had conquered the world but Rome has waned since then, precipitated by the 9-11 attack on the then tallest towers in America, the Trade Center. A malicious sign Rome was in decline. The subsequent wars which followed had no resemblance to the original crime, just an excuse for further global intimidation, the mother load of money. The defense budget in 2001 was 360 billion dollars, today the defense budget is twice that amount. War is big business and politicians can always find a rational to proclaim and continue war. The twenty years from 9-11 has found America, most democratic country in the world, to be corrupted by a history of endemic radical racism from the White People coming from Rome intent on ruling America and through her, the world. However, there is an ancient prophesy about Roman conquest for two thousand years before lying down with the lamb and beating the implements of war into plowshares. That time has come, obvious from the stars in the heavens and the numerous signs upon the Earth. Now that Rome has begun to wane, he will wane forever.

In the year 2003 when America launched their war against the world, the planet Mars came closest to the Earth ever, and the planet Mars will continue to wane forevermore. The last twenty years have been a difficult cusp of change culminating with Covid-19, a world-wide pandemic changing the arc of history, right when Rome thought they had the world sewn up, replete with a history written by the victors. The word Covid in Hebrew has three meanings: Respect, Heavy and Liver; the number 19 has permanent resonance from the 19 hijackers perpetrating the 9/11 attacks used as a justification for the new Christian Crusade against Islam—America has not been a good country. America is a warmonger for the sake of money and power; America exploits poverty and sickness both at home and abroad for money and power—America is the bastion of religion for money and power. America is deemed great for the amount of money in her coffers. The Torah/Teaching of the Jewish People, suggests evaluating people by estimating human worth by a small amount of money, moderately different between man, woman and child, thus putting a cap on money, since the human being is the most precious of commodities in the entire universe.

What is happening in America is heavenly retribution but also Covid-19 is a blessing, saving our society and world from the mechanization of life for purposeless reasons. Limiting human interaction, in lieu of artificial intelligence guiding the hand of robots producing abundance for mass consumption to an addicted population turned dumb. By spinning the world faster and faster propelled by the Big Bang Theory where something comes out of nothing, all sense of morality and Truth are obliterated—"It just is what it is," goes the famous quote from the President concerning the mass deaths in America. A mechanized society requires few people and lots of oil. Money is of paramount importance, thusly way overvalued. The American economy is seventy percent fuel by the consumption from the government and the people. Every aspect of life has been cooped into corporations, from schools to prisons; from hospitals to war—everything is watched and counted as if the populous were slaves. Covid-19 did not come directly from China to America across the Pacific Ocean as might be expected, but rather the disease took a circuitous journey across the western hemisphere until coming to America, the ultimate target, since America is the biggest consumer pushing the world faster. God gave the world Covid-19 to wake up free choice. God is saying, I put before you good and bad, chose good, just as the election looms.

The Human Being on planet Earth needs to ask, Toward what are we progressing and why so quickly? Time is not linear, so by going in a straight line we really get nowhere quickly. Without recognizing the innate curve within the line, man reverts back to the beginning when he was unable to see woman within. Space travel proceeds as a line, the shortest path to the projected spinning future because time is a spiral. The line has no end but the spiral has a conclusion. At the beginning of the spiral, the curve is a large, luxurious in graceful unhurried turns, but by the time the cycle is finished, change happens quickly; in our time, as we approach the fulcrum, life cycles extremely quickly—so fast, some feel the world is ending, but that is not true, only the era of six thousand years of man is ending. A transition to the Thousand Years of Woman and Peace is the future. We are truly going nowhere quickly; societies throughout the world are suffering from the pace of life while a few get rich. In America, the driver of progress and innovation, the populace is pointedly overworked, unsatisfied and unhappy.

The people who lived in the ancient past were primarily spiritual, understanding the cycle of life, able to predict forward into our time. The further back into our ancestry we go, the less physical imprint is made upon the Earth because physicality was merely a thin veneer. After six thousand years, physicality has taken over the body, permeated every cell, trying to push the soul out of the flesh, reflected in society where corporations who have no soul therefore hold no culpability; the corporations have no consciousness and no compassion—the machine has become the master to the inventor who must now feed the machine. The way of the line is a short road which in the end is long because you never get to where you are going; whereas, the long road portrayed by the curve is eventually short, since you actually arrive— the choice facing the world at this important juncture in history is, do we follow the line or follow the curve? The line requires belief in the goal but the curve requires faith in the path. However, the main thing in life is good intention.

Because the phases of the calendar are incorruptible and as one phase ends another begins, the only question is how the story will play out—the free exercise of choice given to the Human Being narrates the story. The Cabala, repository for received knowledge explains, The Creator wanted a dwelling place in Low, therefore time and space were engraved out of the endless possibilities within the Illuminated Singularity, then winnowed down to ten, as represented in the Sun and nine planets, the seven continents and the three oceans and the Human Being built on three triangles plus the power of speech. The seven limbs of the human body: head, torso, arms, legs, sex are reflected in the six outer orbits of our solar system, from Earth to Neptune. Pluto, the final celestial body depicting the ability to articulate thoughts into speech as portrayed in the lips of the mouth, completes the division of 613 into the 248 years Pluto orbits the Sun and the 365 days Earth orbits the Sun, mirroring the 248 limbs of the human form connected through the 365 sinews of the human body, plus the 248 Positive Commandments and the 365 Commandments comprising the 613 Commandments given to the Jewish People in the Torah.

The number seven shows on completeness, in the same way a woman who is depicted by the number seven, completes man. And with all this synchronicity, like the moon precisely covers the sun (if the moon were a bit closer, it would blot out the Ring of Fire around the Sun and if farther away, the Moon would not cover the Sun completely), cutting across the Bible Belt of America, the seat of Rome, in the year 5777, eyes are opening. The Creator's desire to be known in low, in the most corporeal existence at the end of time, is finding conclusion now, 5780 years of reincarnating the human soul, occupying this planet in physical bodies whose DNA produces billions of people, each applying their own unique freedom of choice upon this physical world. Man has the opportunity to culminate or be forever impotent. Once the sperm enters the woman, sex is over and rest begins—a paradigm shift occurring at a cosmic level, now focuses upon Mother Earth, from whence the birth of a new human being will happen because time, like life, is not incremental. Life is a spiral.

As promised by the prophets: In the future, the Earth will give birth to human beings living a thousand years, impervious to sickness or death. Those of us presently living upon the Earth are mankind's lowest denominator; we are the point of the lever inserted beneath the heavy stone called, Purpose, connected to the long rod of human history dating back 5780 years—from us the world will be lifted and turned into the new era. Now is the prelude to the Thousand Years of Woman and Peace. When Trump was elected he was seventy years, seven months and seven days. When the World Health Organizations proclaimed Covid-19 a pandemic on March 11, 2020, there were 7,770,000,000 people in the world. The number 777 represents the Angel of Death. God promised, before the year six thousand, to wipe away the Angel of Death from the world. Donald Trump is the lowest person in the world, a person and family completely bereft of compassion, elevated to the top to be president for the purpose of being cast down by God who can finally be satisfied, having been known in low.

Chapter Three

Another potent sexual metaphor is the relationship between the placenta and the fetus. An ancient knowledge going back four thousand years maintains, life begins 41 days after conception, when the soul enters into the body. During these first forty days, beginning with the insemination of the egg by the sperm, the placenta is grown inside the woman. The placenta, made from the combination of sperm from the father and egg from the mother, grows until the soul enters on the 41st day. Medical doctors recognize this transition at 41 days, making the distinction between the zygote and the fetus. The placenta is the first thing to form and the last to be birthed, hanging on until the very end, even at times obstructing the passage of the child or trying to choke the child rather than confront birth. Despots tend to hold on to power fearing the consequences should they be subjected to the law for their misdeeds. The sole purpose of the placenta is to feed and protect the child while in the gestation process continues but after the child is born, the placenta has no purpose.

When birth happens, a transformation takes place. Prior to birth, the child is fed through the stomach by the placenta, while the faculties of the brain are largely turned off; the eyes do not see, the ears do not hear, and the mouth does not breathe—but, all that changes with birth. The umbilical cord is cut and the placenta is discarded. From the beginning, the placenta knows that birth to the child means death to the afterbirth. The placenta struggles against birth in the same way that the old guard of the world struggles against the end of male dominance, because they fear the death that naturally occurs as a result of birth. The old man dies as the new man struggles to be born. For sake of the metaphor, we can ascribe 1906 when Einstein published the secret of atomic energy, which was the year 5,666, the last occurrence of the 666 in the six thousand year calendar, to be the beginning of the labor process as played out in the two hot world wars followed by a long cold war. By the end of the Sixties came transition, war became reviled throughout the world while an openly public display about sex was underway and a nascent movement for love and equality was slowly gaining momentum.

In 1970/5730, the half life of carbon-14, began the second stage of the birth progress known as, pushing; as a result of the Sixties, there was a push towards the future, being held back by an unseen force—the placenta, also known as the old and foolish king. The struggle to be born beginning in 1970, lasting 42 years, until 2012 when the Mayan calendar concluded a 13,000 year cycle, as our solar system aligned with the center of our galaxy comprising dilation. Each small step forward was met with a contraction pulling back. The number 42 made from six times seven depicts the world of Tohu/Mars called Mob where sexuality was dormant. The Earth, called Tavel, is configured with seven times seven producing 49, the last stage before fifty is achieved. Fifty is forever. The animal inception was in Tohu from where the person receives their animal inclination, having the characteristics from generational DNA implanting an animal personality akin to a particular beast. Animals come and go but to be imprinted forever in Heaven, the human soul, acquired at birth when the eyes open, must first mark the Earth.

The final stage before the actual birth is called, Crowning, when the head of the baby can been seen pushing against the final barrier before birth. Crowning is a sign of imminent birth. These final seven years since 2012 has brought the world to the brink of birth. The world has come as far as she can go and now everything has suddenly halted. Something has to give or the world will die. The system we live within wants to live for its own sake and therefore wants to hold back the evolving human spirit; governments want to recreate the past where money was predominant but that would be like trying to push the baby back into the womb—it is during this time in the birth process when the woman often feels compelled to squat above the ground allowing the child to be born without causing injury to the mother. The midwives who await the delivery caution the mother not to push too fast or breathe too hard; now is the time for a long deep exhale as if blowing out birthday candles. The main thing is, don't freak out. The worst is truly over.

America, famous as being the first country without a king, a country ruled by the people, or so the saying goes. The truth is, America is ruled by certain people whose objectives are questionable. The American system of governance has a lot in common with the placenta trying to hold back birth for his own sake, so he will not die. He does not care about the child being birthed nor the mother whose housing the child, the placenta only cares about himself. The placenta did not feed and care for the child out of love rather as a way of self-adulation. This is where the Angel of Death enters in saying, It is either me or you. This is not a fight to the death but a fight to life. The opposition to life can be traced back to the previous world of Tohu/Chaos also known as Mars, where four thousand years ago man built the Tower of Babel where Avraham was raised. Mars is the ultimate placenta whose cord was cut back in 2003 when Mars came closest to the Earth, ever.

The red planet Mars is god to ancient Rome; modern-day Rome is Caucasian—White Power is Roman Power. Since the year two thousand, Rome has been in decline and like the planet Mars will be in decline forever. Mars is described by the ancients, as a world with a core of ice surrounded by water with a red inhospitable exterior. Water is a sign of kindness as is the color white. As the harsh veneer leaves our world, the essential goodness will be revealed. Rome's spiritual connection is through Avraham, father of the Arab and Jewish Peoples and grandfather to Esau, father of Rome. Esau despised his inheritance and therefore was left without a true spiritual tradition founded in a special language fashioned by Avraham, a master of language. As a result, the ancient gods of Rome were taken from the Greeks and made into Roman gods; Rome shaved the beards from the Greek gods and gave them different names—eventually Rome became fixated on Christianity, the father of all religions. There is no word for religion in Arabic, Hebrew, or Sanskrit because religion is based on a manufactured illegitimate text, The New Testament. The Bible's rendering of the Torah is false from the title, plus their story of Jesus is an uncorroborated racist tale about how the Jews killed god.

Religion is a manmade construct depriving women of their spiritual place within nature, similar to the way male doctors replaced midwives by calling them witches. The patriarchal divisions created by man to rule the world through religion, science, war, economics, institutions and politics have come to culmination in America. America has become the Roman Empire's seat of power. America is the world's bastion of freedom, a land without a king where the baby being born to the world is crowning, how ironic. The Roman Empire never fell, it just morphed into religion and government with banks and a calendar arrogantly going on forever. But, Rome is destined to lie down with the lamb, not to be destroyed. A sign to our time, the time has come to soften Rome, drawing on the real goodness hidden within. Rectifying the harsh waters from Tohu with the kind waters of the Earth has produced life on this planet with the opportunity for the Human Being to make things better, much better. First, to throw off what is wrong then to do what is good. This ancient advice towards repentance fits all times and places.

The eclipse crossing the American Bible Belt on August 21, 2017, on the cusp of Virgo the Virgin, peaked over Christian County, Kentucky, where the great American seer Edgar Cayce lived and practiced. The dark line of the eclipse cutting across America was a sign that the male energies of the world had reached zenith and now will begin to decline. Politics, religion, war, and money will quickly lose their worth, replaced by kinder values. In the manner of the placenta, this male energy wants to hold on and remain dominant beyond the time needed. The transition between male and female is beginning, and just as the sperm quickly dissolves inside the egg, initiating the growth of the placenta which will be discarded when no longer needed, so too will the dominance of male energy. This presumed manifest destiny of man, derived from his dogged determination to dominate, is paramount to male survival—anything less is unacceptable. But, that power to dominate is slipping away, as the six thousand years of male agenda is concluding. After 220 years of transition, time will ultimately be replaced by the Thousand Years of Woman and Peace. When man enters into woman, Pleasure will become paramount around the world displacing Will.

Those pushing progress at a cancerous pace, those fear mongering physicists driving our world into outer space by predicting the Earth will be a dystopian wilderness in a hundred years, are more placenta than Human Being. Nowhere in our universe is there a place like our beautiful Earth dancing in precision with the Moon, the Sun and the stars. The Earth is the fulcrum of life in an embryonic solar system slowly coming into consciousness through our efforts. Those who see the Earth as a rock whose only value is in the metal beaten out of the ground will subjugate the soul for the sake of the ego but eventually will be dragged out into the light of birth and unceremoniously discarded. Inside the womb, the placenta is the captain of the ship, sloshing around in the embryonic fluid of the mother; the placenta delivers nourishment to the unformed child and takes away the refuse—the placenta takes the best from the mother, delivering sustenance to the baby. Also, the placenta infuses the ego into the child; the baby will need that ego for the final rebellion, when the baby gains independence from the placenta—by being born. Birth is life to the child but death to the placenta.

The ancients looked into the future, saw our time and deemed it, Chavalim/Birth Pangs. The male energy surviving birth is subservient to the female. A pregnant woman deserves preferential treatment; in our time, the world is pregnant with women ready to give birth to a new era, a future where human beings grows from the ground out of bone shards from those buried. This new Human Being will be impervious to sickness, living a thousand years; the occurrence of death will be uncommon, happening to children who are a hundred years old—no man on Earth can stop this birth from happening. Those who resist will be left behind and discarded. Generation after generation has refined the soul, allowing it to descend deeper into a lower physical realm, bringing the knowledge of the Creator into the darkness of creation. Donald J.ackassFatass Trump, the lowest person in creation will fulfill God's Desire to be known in low. Trump, a man without compassion, dedicated to money and power is being brought by the scruff of his belligerent neck to bend his knee before the Creator of Heaven and Earth.

Chapter Four

Birth is the result of sex. Sperm can be traced back into Heaven where a tiny essence of the soul is conveyed through the mind, down the spine to the genitals. When Zivug/Sex happens, something is born in Heaven and at times sex results in new life on the Earth. Man makes sperm through his eyes: this is the reason men like to look at women and why women are constantly concerned about being beautiful before men. This primal instinct, carried out in all peoples and cultures is an unpronounceable language, a communication called social intercourse. The eyes derive from and are an expression of the right hemisphere of the brain, where the soul connects with the body. What the man sees makes an indentation in the soul, which in turn activates the production of sperm in the brain. Jewish Law defines sex as when the penis enters into any orifice of woman; men who use condoms are not having real sex—rather, this is a form of masturbation for both the man and the woman. The act of semen entering into the woman evokes a response in Heaven precipitating spiritual birth within the woman, the reason why woman are energized as a result of sex while men are oftentimes drained.

Woman is made opposite of man. She is born with all the eggs, a few thousand for a lifetime, in contrast to man who once into puberty produces sperm without end for his entire life. Because the sperm comes from the mind of man, it is extremely important for man to keep his mind from dwelling on polluted thoughts during sex. Thinking during sex is a distraction, but thinking about something bad or thinking about another woman is much worse since sperm clothed in such thoughts produces spiritual and even physical abnormalities. Man is but a conduit between Heaven and Earth, embodied in the womb of woman after conception as the placenta; the male ego is transferred into the placenta, which decides what goes in and what goes out—he is the keeper of the gate. By the end of nine months, the placenta has become old and caustic; the approaching birth will cause the placenta to be dragged out and discarded—some placentas comply, but others would rather strangle the baby than be born. There are people scattered throughout the world who would prefer everyone die rather than give up their hold on the world.

These cosmic birth pangs began in the year 5666/1906, the sixth millennium since the first Human Being on planet Earth. The Letter Vav/ו-6 is a vertical line indicative of man. Six is the number related to the Letter Vav corresponding to sex through the concept of YeSod/Secret. The number 111 is the value of the letter Aleph/א-1 when spelled out with a gematria 111. Over the past 111 years since the 5666, a pivotal milestone has been reached in 2017/5777. Six is the number of man and seven is the number of woman. The 666 is merging with the 777. And now in 2020/5780, when only 220 years are left until the conclusion of the thousand years dedicated to sex concludes, as the six thousand years of man enters into the Thousand Years of Woman and Peace. The prolific and the destructive are dancing upon the world stage, creating and destroying through the agony of war and the pleasure of opulence. But, now birth is approaching. The sudden lessening of human activity as the world grinds to a halt is measurable. With the onset of the virus, the Earth stopped quaking; the pushing is over, the contractions have ceased—now, just prior to birth is the time to chose between the good and the bad.

Some see the dark side from the virus Covid-19 causing interruption in normality but if we look close, it is easy to behold the beautiful future being ushered in by the disease. Time has come for the paradigm shift. On the shortest day of the year 5772/2012, our solar system crossed over the galactic horizon in the twenty-six-thousand-year cycle around the North Star; the Earth aligned with the very center of our galaxy, achieving dilation forwarding the process of birth—the state of dilation occurs just before the phase, the ultimate push into life. Through nine months of pregnancy, the mother is receptive, sensitive, affable, amenable, but pushing requires the mother to take charge. This internal drama between mother and child, witnessed by those from the outside as moans and screams, are as inauthentic as sex viewed from the outside. The mother must go within, get behind her child and push her baby out through the narrow straits and into the light. This is the long awaited paradigm shift when women become more essential than men.

The transition from fetus to birth is dramatic. The eyes of the child open to a new reality; breathing from the nose and taking in nourishment from the mouth while the stomach closes and the placenta becomes no more than an afterthought, easily cut off and discarded. The metaphor of birth is instructive, particularly in this time of world transition when the globe is pregnant with people while the natural resources of the Earth are being plundered by rich and strident believers in another Roman millennium. Instead, the world is entering a Thousand Years of Woman and Peace. As we slip into the time of woman, man needs to become more attentive. Man's obsession with progress needs to end because the baby is complete. Life is more important than business and money, more powerful than despots with armies or absurd aliens from outer space. Birth awakens love in the hardest of hearts; freshly minted children turn hard hearts into melted butter—a little human being stepping forth from Heaven to Earth. Birth is happening to the entire world and soon, as has been prophesied, a new Human Being will grow from the ground, imperious to pain and disease.

With all their instruments and detection devices, with all the telescopes and rocket ships, the explorers of outer space looking for aliens have yet to understand, our Mother Earth is a living entity in the womb of the solar system embedded within a galaxy spinning on the Finger of God in a universe running toward the OreAinSof/Light-Without End. With all that, God has a special love for the Earth and the life upon the Earth. The eclipse of 5777 was a clear demarcation line beginning the summation of male energy as the female waters rise. The number six corresponds to sexuality, but the number seven is synonymous with woman. The Moon covering the Sun, happening on the cusp of Virgo the Virgin in the year 5777 in the six thousand year calendar is profound. Soon, the Earth will give birth to a new kind of Human Being able to live for a thousand years, fully awakened, composed from all the human beings who came before because life is not linear; life, as does time, spirals down to a crescendo, then opens up into another spiral in the complex weave of creation—all designed from the beginning by the Creator of Heaven and Earth, Melech HaOlam/King of the World.

To better understand the significance to the eclipse of 2017 falling on the cusp of Virgo, it is first necessary to explain how this human calendar later adopted as the Jewish calendar is divided into male and female. The six-month female segment of the year ends with Virgo, beginning the new year in the subsequent month of Tishrei, the beginning of the six male months. Actually, there are four New Years distributed throughout the four seasons mirroring each of the four elements connected to a particular season. In the winter, pleasure is celebrated in water when the sap begins to rise in the trees, along with the sprouting of all growing life; in the spring, air and freedom are celebrated as depicted by the freedom engendered from human speech; summer celebrates the fire and passion of the animal; and in fall, the dirt of the Earth is celebrated from where the Human Being first arose in physical form then forced to breathe when the soul was blown into the man while woman laughed within. The soul filled the form of the body made from dirt, then God took the fire image of the Human Being and brought him to the Garden of Eden to be tested, leaving the human animal to roam the planet Earth.

The Human Being created out of clay requires the three higher, more refined elements to live. The meaning of life, all life, is to come closer to the Creator; the Human Being is the highest life form, but because we are made out of dust from the Earth we can lift the rest of creation higher—in this way, the entirety of creation comes closer to the

Creator through the human acts of kindness. After this final thousand year segment ends in 220 years, the Thousand Years of Woman and Peace will transform life on planet Earth, eventually melding together, one beautiful human soul ready to inhabit another planet. The Earth will repair herself and forevermore will be fecund with life displayed in four seasons over a 365-day revolution around the Sun. The human body composed of six limbs connected to the torso plus speech, is patterned after the outer seven planets; the body is comprised of 248 limbs and 365 sinews according to the Torah/Teaching of the Jewish People. Earth revolves around the Sun every 365 days while Pluto, the seventh planet out revolves around the Sun every 248 years, together equalling 613. The 613 Commandments given to the Jewish People are divided 248 Positive Commandments and 365 Negative Commandments.

Our world is the second in a series of seven sequences of seven thousand years on the seven outer planets: Earth, Mars, Jupiter, Saturn, Uranus, Neptune, Pluto. The process of life began first on Mars, which broke from too much light emanating from Jupiter causing the Asteroid Belt between Mars and Jupiter. From the interior of Mars, this dry planet on the surface suddenly became a gush of water, flooding Earth with the seeds of life having been first incubated within the interior of Mars. There were 288 sparks in all, which came to the Earth inculcating her with life. The nature of the Earth is to grow life, seeds give the direction to the ground as to what to grow. All of life is inculcated with the essence of Tohu/Mars sustaining the animal within, the place where woman was first formed in an atmosphere of independence. There was no need for sex in Tohu but because woman wanted sex, God created man. New to the game of life, man, having been given the keys to the kingdom in a world made for pleasure, immediately did something wrong and when confronted blamed the woman. It took 130 years to migrate back to the Earth, a world called, Tikun/Fixing, fixing the weakness in man.

In this modern era full of gadgets and toys, a strong man uses money and power over other people, but this is a weak man's way. The Torah relates how Moshe instructed spies to assess the strength of the people they were to displace. Moshe, the leader of the Jewish People wanted to know if the enemy lived behind walls or out in the open. Those who live behind walls are considered weak while those who live in the open are strong. American society is ruled by weak people afraid of their own shadow, who require money to enlist soldiers to fight for their cause. Justice only occurs when they win. God is Just, but our world where Truth is reviled for revealing the lie, justice is just a concept. A strong man is an individual who does not need more, he can suffice with what he has; a strong man is not afraid of reality—a strong man knows how to control his sexuality. Strong men do not need to hide behind walls with their gathered opulence having unabated Pleasure. In this world of illusion where the weak appear to be strong, the Truth is hidden. The illumination coming from this newly minted era of light will erase the memory of the past like the sun erases the shadows from the Earth.

Chapter Five

The Sixth Day of Creation, the day on which man was created with woman hidden within, begins the male half of the year from fall until spring. On the first day of the month Tishri, is celebrated the New Year. The ancient names of the twelve months preceded the Hebrew language by two thousand years and are cited in the Epic of Gilgamesh written directly after Noah's Flood. The first word in the Torah is בראשית/Bereshith/In the Beginning. These six letters can be rearranged to read: בא' תשרי/On the First of Tishri. Each yearly cycle is a ring in the Tree of Life, leading to a new year; within each cycle is a unique configuration of stars and celestial contours visited upon the Earth—everything is designed precisely from the beginning, engraved into the firmament sustaining the six thousand years of man. And in each year, the paradigm of male and female is played out by dividing the year of twelve months into two segments of opposite polarity. Each new segment begins with a seven-day holiday happening at the full Moon; on the Eighth Day, the the beginning fall celebration of Succoth, a celestial drop of sperm is emitted, causing conception to take hold, inseminating the New Year.

At the end of the six month male segment birth occurs, beginning the six-month female component during the commemoration of the seven-day exodus from Mitzriam/Constraint—Egypt. Chased by Pharaoh and his army of chariots, like the placenta chases the child, trying to stop the birth, the Jewish People found themselves pinned up against the sea, when suddenly the waters broke, splitting the aqua into twelves paths for the Twelve Tribes, each path filled with miracles. The Jewish People walked along the dry land within the water then back to the shore where the Jewish Nation was born. The army chasing them were destroyed, drowned into the sea. Forty-nine days later, seven weeks are counted until the Eighth Day Holiday. Shavout/Vows, is celebrated on the fiftieth day as a marriage between the Jewish People and the Creator. According to the Jewish Law of marriage, the man must give the woman something of value, before the woman gives herself to the man. The Creator gave two cubes engraved with the Finger of God, the Ten Commandments; the Jewish People gave themselves and their children to the observance and performance of the 613 Commandments embodied in the text of the Torah—produced from the hundreds of thousands of shards in the form of letters comprising the first five books of the Torah.

Later in the summer, on the Ninth Day of Av, the destruction of both Temples is commemorated, five hundred years apart, destroyed on the same day, leading to the exile of the Jewish People. The exile of Babylon lasted for seventy years, but the Roman Exile has continued for two thousand years, during which time Rome, as predicted thousands of years ago, conquered the world. But now, as their patron planet Mars recedes from the Earth, the power of Rome also wanes. This time of the year is considered the divorce, when God burns down the beautiful house where people from throughout the world came to acknowledge the Creator of Heaven and Earth. Six days later, the full Moon of Av is considered the greatest of all holidays for being the Day of Love and the Miracle of Life. There is no prescription or law about how to celebrate this day, known as Tuba Av/15th Day of Av, but the unmarried women had a tradition of exchanging clothes so their status would be indistinguishable; then they would go out into the streets and challenge the young men to marry them—the divorce is over, and now woman returns to her virginal state to end the year, the final month Virgo.

Though each yearly cycle follows the same pattern, each year is different; years become decades and decades turn into centuries—each thousand year segment corresponds to one of the Six Days of Creation.

Spiraling our way into the conclusion of the six thousand years of man necessitates a look backwards to see how we got to where we are. The beginning of life was in long arcs, the effluence of the time was so great that many things could happen in a moment; minutes were like days, and hours were like months—a year was a hundred times fold because time was squared. Creation spiraled out of the heavens, then down to the Earth. The first life on Earth was of high spiritual caliber, knowing the pathways through the heavens but each subsequent generation became lower than the previous generation as our spiritual veneer fell away and the Human Being became more corporeal—man became a harlequin creature caught between Heaven and Earth in an existential crisis for identity. Before the first millennium was even over, people had lost sight of reality and were proposing preposterous theories about how the Creator had created creation and then left, leaving the power to the stars and the constellations.

Like a child without parents, these first human beings knew no bounds; the Seven Commandments given to all peoples through the First Man were ignored—worshiping the stars was more fruitful. Imbued with spiritual adroitness and physical prowess, living for a thousand years, these ardent human beings were like teenage giants. By the year 666, God intervened by taking Chanuch, a righteous man among the wicked and making him into Metatron, Angel of the Earth. All the secrets of time established on the 26,000 year cycle of the Earth appearing to orbit the North Star were given to him, a calendar with an exact beginning and a precise ending date 5,106 years later on 2012 in Roman time. The number 26 is the gematria of the YHVH, the Four Letter Name of God whose letters can be rearranged to make the three tenses of time—היה/Past, הוה/Present and יהיה/Future. Six is the number of sexuality and 666 (6 + 6 + 6) equals 18, the gematria of Chai/Life. The beginning of the Mayan calendar was commensurate with earthly conception, coming to fruition at 5772/2012, the due date when the Earth was aligned with the center of our galaxy. The Mayan calendar ended as the Earth transited the galactic horizon.

As time speeds up, the people of the world are frozen in fear, prompting some devising an escape to a different planet. Time moved much slower back at the beginning, thus much could happen in a short amount of time, but now, as the six thousand years come to culmination, time whizzes by where much is done but at a minute level; like tiny gear in a huge mechanism, technological communication has made the Earth into one body via a conglomeration of electronic brains switching from zero to one—the primal expression of man and woman as depicted by the line and the circle. In this time, progress grows at an unparalleled pace, trying to keep up with the expanding value of money. Yet all of this was set out in the original calendar, starting with the advent of man and ending six thousand years later—220 years from now. Like each primordial day, each thousand year segment has unique characteristics affecting both time and space. History is not linear and each thousand year segment is a progression into the cyclical nature as the spiral begins culmination in our time. Man and God are coming closer through this process dictated by the Six Days of Creation.

On the first day of creation, after 266,450,000 years in preparation (the extrapolated sum deduced from *the two thousand years God played with creation* prior the Six Days of Creation times 365 squared) light becomes tethered to the Earth. During the first thousand years of creation, life on Earth was boundless and people lived for a thousand years, able to navigate through the heavens. On the Second Day of Creation, a division is made in the firmament, the first expression of Gevorah/Severity; at year 1666 the flood came and wiped out terrestrial life. On the Third Day of Creation, God says Ki Tov/It Is Good, twice; the third millennium begins with Avraham coming to the Earth, and through him all peoples are blessed. On the Fourth Day of Creation, the heavens are arranged, corresponding with the calendar of man; in the fourth millennium, two Temples are built in Jerusalem, one lasting 410 years and one lasting 420 years before being burnt to the ground and ending world peace. On the Fifth Day of Creation, life begins in the water, then swarms upon the land; in the fifth millennium the Jewish people begin the long exile into the Roman Empire and beyond.

On the Sixth Day of Creation, man is formed out of clay; by the sixth millennium, the accumulated wealth of the world is in the hands of man. The sixth millennium corresponds to sex, known as YeSod/Foundation based on the word Sod/Secret. In our time and for the past 780 years, the secrets of creation are being exposed; both physical secrets and sublime esoteric secrets are becoming known by everybody, because we are quickly approaching Judgment Day—the day when everything is revealed and we stand in judgment of ourselves as individuals and as a collective. Man, every man in the world, is obligated to stand up and be a man. Man is defined by his actions during this time. Of course, the question is: What is a man? Is there just one type of man? What differentiates men? What about gay men? According to Torah Law, only Jewish men are prohibited from having sex with other men yet, the Torah teaches the greatest love was between two men, Dovid and Yonaton. Lastly, men are commanded to marry and have children but women are unencumbered with these commandments. Women do what they do out of love.

There are four types of men, and each type has a different kind of penis depicting his nature. Adom/One in Blood is the complete man: he has a large penis and when invoked becomes larger. Ish/Man has a large penis but when entreated remains the same. Gebor/Strong has a small penis but when solicited becomes big. Enosh/Weak has a small penis and when beseeched remains small. The penis of the first man lacked a foreskin because the letter Yud, the first letter of the Four Letter Name of God, YHVH, was engraved into the flesh of man in the opening at the end of the penis; however, once having transgressed the Word of God by eating from the Tree of Life, a covering grew over the holy letter—the foreskin. Women have ovaries and men have balls, but the penis is peculiar to man. From the foreskin and the four types of penises a general understanding of who a man is and how to be a man can be derived. One need not be the strongest or the biggest to be a man, because sex is not about size; the virility of a small penis far outweighs the impotence of a large penis—the essence of man is to be a good conduit from Heaven to Earth.

Virility is like a blade of grass pushing through the concrete, nothing stops the perpetual insistence of life. The main thing for man is to stand erect. The ancient wisdom includes this reminder, There is no erection without the knowing of the third eye. A connection between the penis and the third eye may seem like a stretch, but this view is corroborated by the description quoted in the Torah, Man knew woman. This odd nomenclature is adopted because there is no erection without the third eye, the seat of knowing. The seed of man germinates in the brain and is released only when the third eye momentarily opens from the spark of Knowing. Man is the conduit between Heaven and woman; Knowing stops the brain from thinking; the reason behind thinking is to know—knowing is the experience transiting down the narrow of the neck, descending through the spine then cooking in the balls, until finally, after holding back the string of the bow, releasing a torrent of life into woman. Sperm does not enter woman as a stream but rather in spurts, allowing the man the intersession to again drew back the bow before releasing another cluster of arrows, propelled by virility.

However, there is one more aspect to man, his most important ability, the power to Will. Will is the essence of man, while Pleasure is the essence of woman. One is a circle and the other is a line—when the line of the man and the circle of the woman intersect, a spiral is formed. The line of man is directed and strengthened by his Will. A man is obligated through his Will to hold his sperm back as long as he can, to Pleasure a woman. Will and focus stand at man's fulcrum. Virility stems from a strong Will. The nature of Will is to be the rebel; when many Wills align, rebellion happens—without Will, man becomes weak. Will animates man. The job of the woman is to direct the Will of man through the vehicle of Pleasure. A weak man wants to conquer a woman; a strong man wants to Pleasure a woman, because man is a conduit between Heaven and Earth—man needs to stand up erect and know how to direct his Will toward the betterment of woman.

Chapter Six

Male Will is graphically depicted in the erection. Pleasure softens to receive the Will. Man tends to blindly tunnel after his Will, leaving women exclaiming, Men call their penis Dick to be on a first name basis with the one making the decisions. Will is man's essential ability to project into the future, to extrapolate from the present by blocking out everything else but the Will. The goal of Will is to achieve Pleasure; these two chaotic powers, one governing man and the other governing woman, transcend logic—Will and Pleasure are the progenitors of logic. If not directed by Will, logic produces a Will of his own, according to what pleasures can be derived logically. Desire for money is driven by Pleasure but money has no intrinsic value, particularly American currency which is the empty promise of a government gazillions of dollars in debt. True Will comes from the soul, illuminating a path through life, clarifying distinctions until the goal becomes fastened to the post at the far end of a tightrope; with eyes affixed on the prize, nothing else matters—Will is the essence of man, a straight line to what is wanted but life is a narrow bridge, the main thing is not to be afraid.

Will and Pleasure animate sex, replicated in the temporal renderings of the third eye. The power of Knowing plus the power of Will and Pleasure are interchangeable attributes. Knowing, a result of logic, is beyond logic; we do not know how we know because Knowing quits the mind from thinking—Knowing connects the head to the heart. The first man and woman knew each other, meaning they had sex. This strange nomenclature relates to the inner escapade of sex; beyond the physical manifestation of flesh—is the ethereal experience of Knowing. The entire reason for thinking is to eventually know something.

When the mind intercedes with a manufactured will, not the real Will coming from beyond logic, then Knowing is bypassed, causing the heart to ignite with false intention. Man's seduction of woman happens when a man has false intentions; he has false intentions because his will is manufactured by his ego—as opposed to being a proper conduit for his soul. Love that lasts forever is a love without a reason; love dependent on rationale is gone when the reason leaves—Knowing is twofold, either we love or we hate.

Love and hate are the two extremes manifested by primordial Will and Pleasure. The soul's directives enter into the right side of the brain, initiating a light called Mah/What with a gematria of 45—the present president is the 45th President of the United States, and no wonder for four years everyone is scratching their heads, saying the same thing, What? The right side of the brain sparks questions inside the mind ignited by the soul, provoking an energy between the two hemispheres of the brain, Mother and Father each thinking differently. This inner process is extrapolated into social intercourse and dating. At some point during the dating process, the partners come to a conclusion—they know. Perhaps they know they are in love, or perhaps they know they are going to have sex—but no matter the conclusion, the thinking process ends with Knowing. When Knowing is achieved, the barriers come down and the heart becomes exposed. The heart relies on the head for protection, like a woman relies on a man for protection; the head sees, hears, smells and thinks—when the head knows, then the heart opens.

When people harbor hidden agendas, particularly people in government, it is commensurate to implanting a fabricated will made to circumvent Knowing. The government is the head and the American People are the heart, in a world feeding off falsehoods. The head has tremendous power over the body because, besides housing the brain, the head also possesses the built-in faculties of sight, sound, smell, and speech. The job of the head is to safeguard the heart; the heart is a bastion of emotions responding to input from the brain—the heart depends on the head to communicate truthfully to the heart. Emotions are predicated on Knowing. Once the emotions know to either love or hate, along with all the subtle nuances involved in communication, the emotions begin to emote. The six emotions, corresponding to the first Six Days of Creation, each day corresponding to a thousand years of subsequent history, are considered man, compared to woman, who is seven. The first distinction between these two divisions called, Mother and Father, corresponds to the mental interaction between the two hemispheres of the brain producing the mind.

The six emotions plus speech correspond to sexual union, called Man and Woman, the male-female paradigm. Looking at the entire human form, the head is male, and the torso plus limbs are female. Animals walk on all fours with head and heart at the same elevation, meaning the head is there to satisfy the heart since they are both on the same level. But in the erect human stature, the head is purposed to protect the heart, so the emotions can be true. The heart is crucial since the heart connects directly to the Creator, similar to how the soul connects directly to the Creator, while the head is stuck between the heart and the soul—furthest from the Creator, thereby freeing Free Will in the absence of light. Earth occupies the lowest place in creation, and modern man is the lowest human form who comprehends the least amount of light and therefore has unrestrained Will. Man is the mirror reflecting light back to the Creator; surrounded by woman and the soul, man's job is to recognize the Creator and sublimate his own ego—the sense of importance embodied in the I. By man learning to be a conduit from the soul to the woman, Will transmutes the I into We.

America is based on, We the People. The government has taken on the mantle of man depicted as the head, while the People of America are treated like subjugated women. In the Thousand Years of Woman and Peace, men will protect and respect women instead of being domineering and deprecating like the politicians who currently run America, the modern seat of the Roman Empire. The revolution happening in America and throughout the world is erupting from the quiet and modest demands of the past; determined, like a blade of grass unimpeded by the thickly paved asphalt of assholes—the People are rising. Nothing can stop the birth of the new Human Being. We are all part of the story, the culmination of the Six Days of Creation happening now, in our time at the juncture of 5777 at the cusp of Virgo crossing the Bible Belt of America with an eclipse of the Sun by the Moon, a celestial sign. The day the president was swore into office, he was seventy years, seven months and seven days, is another celestial sign. On March 11, 2020, the World Health Organization proclaimed Covid-19 a worldwide epidemic, there were 7,770,000,000 people in the world, a third sign.

Male Will, with a penchant for conquest, an ambition for subjugation, virulent with all means of destruction, obliterating peace throughout the world, needs spiritual purpose. Implanted within each sperm is the instinct to battle; all the countless sperm fight with one another, testing their strength like bees after the queen—men are like that, always pushing each other. The test is about more than who is strongest—clarity, stamina, integrity are some of the virtues that stem from battle. The job of man is to be a conduit for life, filtering spiritual light through a clean, strong vessel. In every generation, through the six segmented thousand year timeframes dictated by the Six Days of Creation, there has always been these four types of men. The strong man is the viral man who knows how to hold back what he has to give until the proper time. Weak men are cruel and deprecating to women. Many weak men reincarnate as women because they have been cruel to women in a previous lifetimes. Like all the attributes of the body, the essential energies of Will and Pleasure are neither right nor wrong, how we use them and the intention applied is much more important.

But beyond Knowing and even beyond Will is intention. God does not judge the Human Being according to some law or whether the person did right or wrong—God judges the person according to their intentions. Only God knows the intention in each heart. Lies are meant to cover bad intentions, but no one can lie to God who sees all but remains silent. The relationship between God and the Human Being on planet Earth has been depicted by the ancients as two lovers exploring the delights of being in love. God loves all creation; the true Pleasure of life is the love between the human soul invested in the physical body devised by our Creator—spoken from the heart. But, love is temporal, particularly in this false world where true intentions are hidden; a wrong intention wanders away from the true path to follow a manufactured desire or chase anger—suddenly God is gone, then loneliness and despair step in. God is never truly gone because God is everywhere, all the time, to everyone, but God can turn God's Back. There are three types of relationships: front to front, front to back and back to back. When we turn our back to God, then God's Back is turned to us.

God's love is forever, as is the patience of the Creator; however, life has a script with six acts culminating at an exact time revolving around six and seven. Every six concludes with a seven; the six emotions desire to be expressed in the world through action—the most unique attribute of the Human Being to our ability to articulate thoughts into feelings then spoken into the wind of the world, each voice an instrument in the symphony of human expression. The freedom of choice bestowed on the Human Being refers to how much we want God to be in our story, which determines how much we are in God's story, The Story of Creation. In the Creator's story of creation, God sees the human soul within the Singularity and makes room for the soul projected into the emptiness of space from a beam of light boring into the illumination—leaving the soul expressed in the lowly realm of time. Once disconnected from the Singularity, the soul is able to have self-awareness within the gross nature of creation, but this is not enough for the Creator who wants to known in low.

At the bottom of creation is the universe, where the spiritual world is broken into four categories: black hole, galaxy, solar system and Earth. The universe is the realm of the angels and the final resting place for the human soul, from where migration to and from the Earth is possible—physicality is the lowest place in creation. Besides creating creation for the soul to know existence, God also had an unfulfilled desire: God wants to be known in Low, so God created time and space culminating with the Human Being on planet Earth with enough free choice to disavow the existence of the Creator—now, that is low. Women commune from their heart, which is connected directly to God; men, who are stuck between woman and their soul, are at the lowest place in creation—men are the lever placed at the bottom of creation, able to lift up the entire universe. Therefore, Jewish men are obligated to perform the 613 Commandments divided up into 248 of commission and 365 of omission. Women are exempt from all of the positive commandments related to time, while the rest of the world relies on the Seven Commandments of Noah. Only Jewish men, because of our lowly statue in creation, are required to perform all 613 Commandments.

Chapter Seven

This division of 613 into 248 and 365 is mirrored in the orbits of the Seven Heavens through the Earth's 365 days rotation around the Sun plus Pluto, the seventh planet out from the Earth sporting a 248 years rotation around the center of our solar system. Spiritual life abounds on the seven outer planets, which correspond with the seven parts of the human body: head, left and right arms and torso, right and left legs and sex. The Jewish People are pulling on a rope made of 613 strands suspended between Earth and Heaven, to bring light to the world so God can be known; the human body can also be divided into 248 limbs and 365 connecting sinews—the sex of the body is called Sod/Secret. We have completed 777 years into the thousand years corresponding to the Sixth Day of Creation, when the Human Being was fashioned out of clay. Now is the time, all secrets are spilling forth in every aspect of life, from politics to astronomy, from the spiritual to the mundane; each person has a social-media profile shared with the rest of humanity—everything is being revealed and in the end, clarity will replace the darkness.

In lovemaking, the intention of the heart is revealed beyond the capacity of the mind to hinder expression: grunts and groans, hard breathing, erratic exclamations are the language of sex—a primitive animal language meant to break any semblance of correctness. In Jewish Law, where there are laws without end, there is no law about how to conduct sexuality between a man and a woman. Sex is beyond mind and heart; sex is about action, steered by Will and Pleasure, fueled by emotions—sex happens at the horizon of Heaven and Earth. The repository of sperm is in the head, but sperm's essence is in the intention engraved into the heart. God judges the world on our intentions. God loves creation, but for creation to love God requires acknowledgment that God the Creator is available to all creation, all the time, everywhere. Creation was made for love and Pleasure because creation is a love story between the Creator and the Human Being. The Baal Shem Tov, a famous Jewish mystic, was asked, "How to love God?" The Baal Shem Tov replied, "Love what God loves." God loves creation, and creation needs to love back, like the Moon adorned with the light from the Sun reflected upon the Earth.

The most miraculous part of an eclipse is the precision with which the Moon covers the Sun. If the Moon were a little farther from the Earth, her circumference would be unable to cover the disk of the Sun; similarly, if the Moon were a bit closer to the Earth, she would blot out the Sun completely. The Moon is precisely at the right place for a total eclipse, allowing the measurements of light rays as they bend around the Moon. Einstein predicted this phenomenon, proving light was more than just a ray void of substance; there is a relationship between the Sun and the Moon—thus the photon was discovered. The Moon had been holding place until God took a pebble from beneath the Kesey HaKoved/Honored Chair, wrapped the stone in layers then placed the stone in place of the Moon, who had her own light in the beginning. Seeing the two orbs of Sun and Moon were precisely the same, the Moon complained to the Creator, "There can not be two kings!" So, God suggested to the Moon to be passive. That is how the Moon became Queen so the Sun could be King.

The Sun and Moon have a relationship, and the precise way they fit together is a sign from what is written in the Torah, God made two large luminaries; one large light ruled the day and the other large light ruled the night adorn with stars. God put the stars in the orbit of the heavens to shine upon the Earth. The Creator placed the Sun and the Moon precisely where they needed to be for the Moon to perfectly eclipse the Sun when viewed from the Earth. The Sun and the Moon are mother and father looking down upon their infant child; the seven continents like the seven parts of the human body are floating in the womb of three oceans—beneath two orbs, equal in significance, having opposite natures. The sun revels in giving equally to everyone and everywhere without judgment; generosity at the ultimate level is embodied by the Sun—the brightness of kindness can blind the eye. The Moon has the opposite nature. Having no source of her own light, the Moon must first receive and then reflect the light from the Sun down upon the Earth. The family of man on the Earth has a Mother and Father in the heavens.

The Moon has phases. At times she gives no illumination; two weeks later, she is pregnant with a belly full of light, sometimes the Moon waxes and sometimes the Moon wanes—the Moon is always different, she is never the same. Most calendars are regulated by the phases of the Moon. The Sun is full of ego; when the Sun shines, everything else pales—the stars disappear as the Moon shrinks into a white haze. But when the brightness of the Sun disappears at nightfall, the Moon and the stars show a different face of reality; the immense span of creation is seen only in darkness—we can bathe in the light of the moon, we can look upon her beautiful face and lap up the stars from the Milky Way. As a reward for making herself small, the Moon was adorned with a plethora of stars; the Sun and the Moon are precisely the same size as viewed from the Earth—the two largest orbs in the sky hovering over the only planet in the Universe fecund with life. Ancient peoples prayed to the Sun and the Moon and had the ability to manipulate the star beams, manufacturing what they wanted. Idolatry is stealing the light from Heaven without permission.

The idea of a cosmic Mother and Father is also reflected in the relationship between the planet Mercury and the Sun; the relationship between the largest and smallest cosmic bodies, also the closest in proximity to one another, is representative of the two hemispheres of the brain—Venus is the third eye. The seven outer planets of our solar system correspond to the past six thousand years and the thousand years in the future as depicted by the seven parts of the human body.

We stand upon the crux of that division between six and seven, the transition from the darkness of ego into the light exuding human kindness—the merging of man and woman. Male energy has been transformed into a graphic display of opulence, in which only the rich survive and the poor die. But the red sky will quickly fade and turn grey as the world moves into a kinder time. The prelude to the Thousand Years of Woman began in earnest with the eclipse of 5777/2017, a harbinger of the future when the 777 would be revealed three years later through Covid-19. This transformation is aped by the ejaculatory manner from the current president, promising the biggest and best of everything is about to come.

In the same way, the brightness of the Sun obliterates the universe, man has despoiled the Earth through power and conquest blinded by is own light, unable to see woman. The ancients called Blindness, Sogi Ore/Too Much Light. Male power and Will have eradicated all other options, but as the Sun is setting on this Sixth Day of Creation, it becomes incumbent upon man to become a good lover of life through peace and respect. One of the prophesies concerning the End of Days, our time, is the Moon will be bright like the Sun. When the six thousand male years finally ends, the Moon will shine a kind light upon the world in the Thousand Years of Woman and Peace. One of the more subtle ways of hampering this transition from happening is through the calendar continually counting Roman time which was over twenty years ago. These are the End of Days because this is the end of the calendars: carbon-14, Roman calendar, Mayan calendar and in 220 years the end of the six thousand year male calendar. The job of man, in this time, is to make the Earth a good place for women, because the birth of a new era, a paradigm shift, is upon the world.

For man to be complete and for the consummation of the day to become whole, man must merge with woman like day inevitably slips into night. The worldwide phantasmagoric orgasm brought on by too much indulgence in physical pleasure and power is a premature ejaculation. The Moon guides the rays of the Sun to enter into the quiet of the Earth. The Moon made herself small so the Sun could expose, expand

and fix the ego, but now the time of man is ending, the Sun is setting and rest is in the future. In the future there will be no more teachers, because everyone will see with clarity the Truth of creation, each with a unique perspective. The majority will no longer rule—the individual will rule in cooperation. In the future, each person will be a rebel, but there will be no rebellion; man will not rule over man, and flesh will no longer need to protect flesh. Eventually, male and female will become one again, an androgynous being, as was the first man/woman 5,780 years ago. Though love is primal to creation, people who think life is just about love are often the same people who out of frustration, think there is no purpose in creation other than love.

Without purpose, all that is left is love and fear. The purpose of creation is get closer to the Creator, love is but one aspect of that goal. Since God is neither physical nor spiritual, God interacts with creation through two Names: one male, the YHVH; and the other female, Elohim. These two Names are as a spiritual Father and Mother to creation, plus they have a Daughter named Shekina/Presence. Every seven days the Presence of God upon the Earth rises up to merge with the YHVH who descends, considered a celestial marriage, the Shabbat, Day of Rest. From the Shabbat comes the blessing for the new week. During the 24 hours of the Shabbat there are four times of prayer each comprised of seven blessings. The first three prayers are said at night, in the morning and at around noon. These three session of seven prayers make 777 which constitutes ending. The last prayer in late afternoon is the blessing for the coming week encapsulated in the last prayer of seven blessings. The Talmud-Book of Law goes so far as to say, All sevens are beloved; the sevens referred to, are the seven latter components of the Tree of Life representing emotions—embedded in the Ten Sefirot/Luminaries.

The human form is configured according to the Tree of Life—it is built from three triangles corresponding to the head, torso, and hips with their extensions of arms, legs, and sex. The seventh attribute is the power of speech—speech is made from five components: throat, palate, tongue, teeth, and lips. The outer seven outer planets of our solar system represent this configuration, spanning the number 248; Pluto, the seventh planet from the Earth and the last of the ten celestial bodies of the solar system, represents speech—Pluto has five Moons corresponding to the five elements of speech. Pluto and the Earth have similar topographies since each represents seven; on Earth there are seven continents and the year was 5777 when the eclipse of the Sun by the Moon crossed America, the Throne of Rome, right through the Bible Belt because the transition between six into seven has begun in this country, a country who has never had a king other than the Creator, who is King over creation. To know how to accomplish merging six into seven, we must look to the Creator for instruction, because this phenomenon has never happened before. The world is a pregnant woman about to give birth to her first child.

Chapter Eight

There is an ancient story passed down in the Talmud about a teacher who awoke one morning to find one of his students hiding beneath his bed. When the teacher inquired of the student, why he was beneath his teacher's bed, the student replied, "You taught me that I should learn everything from my teacher. I wanted to know about sex, so I hid beneath your bed to learn about sex."

The teacher, confounded by his student, asked, "Well, what was it like?"

The student answered, "It was like hearing a person eating chicken for the first time."

Sex is about working the fertile furrows of the flesh before planting the seed produced in the essence of the mind, connected to the vitality of the soul. There are no rules or confines when it comes to sex, when reality collides with pretense. There is an animal component to sex, enough to get us out of our brains and into our bodies, but the inner aspect of sex is where the true longing resides. So soon the flesh grows numb as the appetite of the eyes are gratified, but the longing of the soul knows no limit, because satisfying a spiritual longing with physical Pleasure is impossible. Without question, sex is the Creator's Tool employed in making creation, using the polarities of opposites to create a dualistic world. Even the Names are utilized for spiritual sex; the Shekina hovers upon the Earth while the YHVH, known as Kodesh/Separate from Creation, interact as man and wife during the twenty-four hours of the Shabbat. The YHVH seeds Shekina with the essence of life so she can return to the world with new blessings for creation. The commandment to keep the Shabbat is twofold: Shomir/Watching and Zakor/Doing.

The prohibition to the Jewish People against working on the Shabbat is fortified with the obligation to have Pleasure—also, moving fire is prohibited. The Zohar explains, No foreign fire should be mixed with our passion for the Creator, like a man having sex should not think about another woman. Given these three primal elements: work, Pleasure and fire, is key to understanding spiritual sex. The Pleasure involved in work is nothing compared to the Pleasure of having finished work; resting after completion is the greater Pleasure—nothing is greater than Pleasure. The Shabbat celebrates the Seventh Day of Creation, when the Creator rested after completing the Human Being on planet Earth along with the accompanying animals and plants, all connected to beams of light from the stars regulated by the Sun and the Moon. Without the finality of rest, work is never finished; the Pleasure in completion is like none other—for twenty four hours, every seven days, Creator and creation merge in completion. For 3,500 years, every seven days, the Jewish People celebrate this holiday through food, wine, and sex, while refraining from work. The Talmud-suggests, If a person is going to have sex once a week, it should be on Shabbat night.

Introducing a strange fire into the fabric of the universe to compete with the passion from the Names of God is not a good idea. During the Shabbat, the world reverts to woman, to receiving without thought or worry, indulging in all sorts of hedonistic pleasures for the purpose of rejuvenation. Pleasure is the essential element of life for which all living creatures crave; living is not enough to sustain life—without Pleasure, life withers and dies. Sex, the progenitor of life, is the greatest of all Pleasure. The Shabbat is a day of royalty beneath a woven crown from Will and Pleasure. The male and female expressions of essence in a dualistic world where even the essence is dualistic. In this dualistic creation, God is One. Creation is dualistic because everything physical or spiritual can be broken down and divided. Since God is One and not dualistic, God can be everywhere to everybody all the time. Creation only exists to satisfy God's Will to be known in low. The Pleasure God takes from each individual using freedom of choice to navigate life enlivens creation. The first of the 613 Commandments is, To know God. When we know God, then God is known in low, but the question is, how low does God want to go?

The most important part of the Seventh Day is the beginning. The separation between work and rest happens when the Sun sets, but it is imprudent to wait until the last moment; the Jewish custom is to light candles eighteen minutes before sunset—adding onto the Shabbat a number, חי/18/meaning, life composed of three sixes. Similarly, when observing our own span of time at the end of the six thousand years of man, whose splatter of color, painting the sky portending climax quickly turns gray. Trump represents a premature ejaculation of the unrestrained purposeless endeavors of mankind ending in impotence. The eclipse of 2017 across the Bible Belt of America in the year 5777 begins the prelude to the Seventh Day of Creation when the Creator rested. Time to stop, clean up the house, shower and change clothes because the Shabbat is coming. Now is the time when real men step forward and take charge; men who know the meaning of life, who cherish each soul embedded in flesh harboring an essential piece of the puzzle fulfilling the Will of God, Melech HaOlam/King of the World—no one knows what is small or great in the eyes of the Creator.

The Rabbis suggest prayer and study as paths by which we enter the spiritual realm and receive the effluence from the Creator in a pure state during the Shabbat; yet the same Rabbis also say that if a man has sex once a week, that day should be the Shabbat. Sex requires preparation beyond foreplay, so the afterglow of sex can be a delicious rest. He who does not work before Shabbat is unable to rest on the Shabbat. What we do on the Earth has ramifications beyond the universe, even into the endless realms beyond the spiritual, to the inner essence of creation. Because God wants to be known in low, we on the Earth have direct communication with the Creator. Once in Heaven, because of the penetrating light, the soul becomes blind to God and only sees illumination, while here on Earth we must peer through the darkness, drill into the hard stone of living, be a broken bit stuck in a hard place, frustrated with anger, learning tenacity and patience to finally achieve a glimmer of the benevolent light coming from the source. There is no question, life on Earth is difficult for everyone. Hidden difficulties are love packages sent from the Creator through the heavens for a reason. But, sex makes it all worthwhile.

The source of sex is found in the number six. The occurrence of sex in the cosmic coming of age was five thousand years ago, in the first occurrence of the year 666. The five thousand year Mayan calendar embedded within the six thousand-year human calendar, representing the beginning of the human gestation of the future man through the subsequent five millennia. On December 21, 2012, when the Mayan calendar ended, the Earth was located directly opposite the center of our galaxy, the Milky Way, passing through the galactic horizon—an event that happens only once every 13,000 years. This momentous occasion coincided with the human calendar at 5772; the number seventy-two is indicative of the essence of the Human Being and is the gematria of the word, חסד/Kindness. The four years and four months spanning the end of the Mayan calendar in 2012 to the eclipse of 2017 is an ephemeral connection between these two dates. An intervention of four often happens between events. There are seven Names of God, the first and last Names are of four letters, like the four dimensions of creation, the four elements, four directions because the world is forever four.

The significance of this event, breaking the constancy of male energy in the year 5777/2017 on the cusp of Virgo, was enough to shift the entire world toward the coming Thousand Years of Woman and Peace by electing Trump as President of the United States of America, the richest and most powerful country in the world. As proof to this assertion when Trump was inaugurated he was seventy years, seven months and seven days. On March 11, 2020 the day the World Health Organization proclaim Covid-19 to be a pandemic, there were 7,770,000,000 people populating the world. The 777 is an ancient sign of the Angel of

Death because everything concludes in seven. Added together, the 777 equals 21, the gematria of God's futuristic Name known as אהיה/I Will Be. The juncture to make this dramatic change is now. A leap into the paradigm shift is inexorably happening. America is like a little world since America is composed of peoples from throughout the world, in a country never before ruled by a king; America is based on freedom of expression but also a powerhouse of prosperity—America was but a young virgin woman when discovered five hundred years ago.

America was taken by Rome through wars of conquest with various Roman factions before decimating the native population who thought it absurd to sell the land which belonged to the Creator. Manhattan was purchased with a bag of common stones and beads, the original scam, thinking they could sell something not belonging to them, like the Brooklyn Bridge. After this ignominious beginning, America begun the importation of black slaves. The Holy Roman Catholic Church preaches until today their religious dogma proclaiming, Black People are cursed to be slaves, along with Jews being cursed because they murdered god and of course Rome's proclamation reviling the hated homosexuals. America was formed with a constitution based on the Iroquois Confederacy, beginning with 13 colonies. The number 13 is the gematria אחד/One. Eventually the entire country was divided up into states who fought a civil war to establish and protect the unity of the nation. America grew towards freedom; a hundred years ago women and minorities won the right to vote. The advent of women into politics caused a seismic shift towards equality, yet a hundred years later, Americans are still filling the streets demanding freedom and equality while the world looks to America for direction.

The word America can be broken down in two Hebrew words, Am/Nation and Ryka/Empty. The Talmud teaches, An empty vessel is a strong vessel. America's true strength is in her ability to return to her virginity, to her emptiness, ready for a new man, in the same way the month of Virgo, Besula/Virgin, precedes the New Year. America needs to speak to the world, to give direction and assume a global leadership role because America is a little world. The upcoming historic election for president is a turning point in the span of American history and world history. However, this election is also spiritually important because a clear choice is being offered between good and bad; between life and death—chose life, is the advice given from the Torah written 3500 years ago. Freedom of choice in a country with free expression at the End of Days between the juncture of man and woman, life and death—what could be more poignant? This is what is known as Judgment Day; it is not the People who are judged but the People who stand in judgment of arrogance, deception and perfidy.

We live in a perfect storm of numbers, like a clock slowly ticking away the moments to an extraordinary opportunity, changing the world by defining the future through how we conceive of the Creator. Did the Creator create creation then leave the working to stars or is the Creator here? Each person partakes in the pleasures of life, producing a unique experience offered up to the Creator, whether sour or sweet, both are delicious to the Creator who created us. Everything is paid for in karma; all deeds are written into the Book of Life—now is the time to chose.

Chapter Nine

From the Earth to the Moon is a great distance, and the celestial grace shown by the Moon on the Earth is seen in the tides of the succulent sea, rushing against time—the inevitable destiny coming to the Earth. The years of man and woman are chapters in the Book of Creation, divided up into six thousand years of man and concluding with the Thousand Years of Woman and Peace. The enmity between the sexes has existed since the beginning, causing an expansiveness of sexual expression, from androgyny to asexuality—sex is a truly an individual, unique experience. There are no laws or restrictions governing the expression of sexuality. Even the restriction written in the Torah against homosexuality is only directed at Jewish men, not Jewish women and not any other males in the world. Religion has skewed the truth causing governments to enact unfair and immoral laws governing private actions. Normal sexuality is just a place on the bellcurve. Heterosexuality, homosexuality, bisexuality, asexuality, polysexuality, pansexuality, transsexualism are all considered valid expressions of love, not to be judged or denigrated because the experience of sexuality is undefinable. There is no standard nor limit, sexuality goes on forever combining the finite with the infinite.

Sex is a Godly act because God likes sex; when engaged in sex, the common refrain is often, God or Oh my God—sex gets right to the point, immediately. But because sex is undefined, amorphous and without regulations, sex is often subject to misuse and manipulation. According to Jewish Law, men who seduce women are considered thieves, since women are particularly susceptible to speech and easily swayed; seduction is a subtle type subversion and theft—lying to women is disrespectful. A man should say the truth but in a gentle, respectful way. God gives the Ten Commandments to the Jewish People in two voices identified by two ways of speaking: Debair/Spoke for the men and the more gentle Amor/Spoke for the women. The seducer proclaims his false emotions to be true, thus stealing the trust of the woman. The seducer knowingly pretends and if successful the woman, Gets Fucked. This famous four-letter word, ubiquitous around the globe, has a pervasive spiritual meaning—a word opposite to God's Four-Letter Name, YHVH. When these four Hebrew letters of God's Four Letter Name are stood vertically, they form a stick figure of the Human Being, who was made to love; however, when dishonesty creeps into a relationship, sex turns into Fucking—Fornication Under Consent of the King.

In ancient times, societies were built on the relationship between the people and royalty; in our times, when the reverence for monarchy is merely ceremonial, the people of a country or even just a city are reliant on government, running on politics. Politics is the science of the lie. No wonder we all feel fucked. The natural waning of male energy is being covered up and manipulated through lying and bullying trying to seduce the people back into their fold of false promises. The relationship with a true king who is crowned by the people forged in love is higher than any government, trusted and revered, the king commands and the people respond. We see what governmental freedom has produced, a lot of things no one needs, terrible waste and pollution plus constant war. A king who loves his people and land would never decree such corruption—off with their heads. The time of kings is over, but Melech HaOlam/King of the World is never over. True freedom is to have a king who draws boundaries and proclaims times, so the people can be free within the confines of love, with a common parent to all.

Our planet is made to support our species, melded from animal body and human soul into one flesh. Woman connects with the spirit of nature since woman goes in, whereas man connects with the coarseness of the ground where the animal runs wild. Woman tames man. But in our time, as the man in charge comes to the culmination of his premature ejaculation, which is a sign of weakness, Donald Trump is leading the charge. This errant male energy has climaxed by shooting rockets up into space in a pointless attempt at progress. They are impotent and ineffectual. A strong man holds back and waits for woman, for the feminine waters to rise. Man has made things and gone places, but what is the motivation behind his actions? Men are meant to be heroic, to give up their lives for ideals. They stand before the adversary, protecting the women and children—man with his Will can do anything, but what is his intention? Intention is the source of motivation; intention is the premise, the seminal seed to all that follows, therefore—God judges the Human Being replete with free choice by our intentions not our choices. What is chosen is only a stab into the refracting waters of time and space.

In the beginning of human history, man was ejected from the Garden of Eden because he tried to wipe his hands on woman, claiming, "She gave me the apple and I ate." These male endeavors, such as business, government, and particularly religion, have made wiping their hands on the People, an institutional strategy. Businesses are constantly passing on the price of doing business to the consumer while using their stockholders to justify their philosophy of the bottom line business; in turn, the stockholders give the CEOs vast salaries to exploit implicit greed—governments protect the rich blaming the poor, taking away the benefits from working people earned by being productive cogs in society, so America can buy more fucking bombs. Religion sells Heaven blaming the people for their sins, while businesses sell the impossible satiation of desire. These are all weak male attributes mired in distrust, lies, and other malefactions—all three: business, government, and religion have one fear in common, the individual. It is difficult to be a man and not be usurped by other men, or even worse, find a woman to hide behind because life is hard. God made life hard for a reason.

There is a loneliness in being a man to which many men succumb; but men are meant to be alone, reflecting our place at the bottom of creation—furthest from the Creator. Only where the light of creation is hidden, can freedom of choice be revealed. A child does not have freedom of choice until puberty, but is not judged by Heaven until the age of twenty when life begins to be counted in decades. Judgment Day is not about God judging man, but about man judging man. Those who maintain that time is endless will never accept judgement, but those who understand the segmentations of time will also understand the importance of conclusion and a final evaluation before entering into the Thousand Years of Woman and Peace. Only through an honest evaluation can the problem be corrected. Correcting man's influence in the world by applying the curve to the line is necessary and inevitable. The line of man needs to be curved by the influence of woman. When the line resists the curve is when the Will of man overshadows the ultimate Pleasure from life. The curve sways the line into a spiral heading into an objective.

Women cycle through lifetimes of incarnations as circles, always new and different, but man is a line, picking up after each lifetime where he left off. The six thousand years of man have a similar configuration and nature; now, at the End of Days, end of the calendars, the line is finally concluding as man merges into woman, as the line entering the circle completes the spiral. Now is the time to take stock of who and what man is, since now is the final judgment before being forever cast as the immutable man. A person is judged at the end of life to determine their place in Heaven; the judgment coming at the End of Days will define man forever—both metaphors of sex and birth are relevant during this strident time. Deceptive thinking is not helpful during times of necessity. America has fallen into the allure of the lie and the mirage giving temporal respite from the truth. Now is the time to perfect man, not through action but through intention. A God inspired revolution is occurring throughout the world begging the question, what do we want in the future?

In the beginning, God gave man a present, a beautiful woman to be his mate; but man had a weakness: he could not admit he was wrong and instead blamed the woman. Certainly, in our time, a new evaluation of life on planet Earth is necessary. Obviously, man has disrespected woman, our beautiful gift from the Creator. The simple truth is, if woman is happy then man is happy, and if the world is happy, God is also happy. All peoples share the same desire to have a mate and perhaps a family, but this basic, ubiquitous dream has been thwarted by man's schemes to make money by subjugating the masses for the purpose of world domination and outer-space exploration. We must be mad. This insensitivity to the gentler gender is a direct result of male institutions. Now is the time to rectify what we have done wrong by focusing on the needs of woman rather than the wants of man. The dominion of woman extends to our lush planet, which has been disrespected over the centuries as man spills the blood of her children throughout the globe and fouls the water and soil, leaving the animals without resource. No wonder God sent us a cure called, Covid which means Respect in Hebrew.

The first man was made androgynous, but the male part could not see the female, so the Creator first had to separate them, so man could see woman. Now, even after 5,780 years, man still does not see woman. Man is not greater than woman, nor are men and women equal; rather, man needs to hold woman above himself, so woman can crown the man. Though Jewish women are exempt from all of the positive commandments related to time, there are a few notable exceptions. Just prior to the setting sun of the sixth day in the week, as the Shabbat enters into the world, Jewish women light the Shabbat candles, bringing the glow of the Shekina, the feminine presence of God, into the world. Though the Shekina is always present, on the Shabbat She is revealed. Shekina is very gentle and quiet, but most of all She is modest. Sometimes inadvertently, we kick the Shekina, enraging God. So, on the Shabbat when She is revealed on this low gross plane, we must be particularly diligent about actions and even thoughts. With the power of seven, the Shabbat is able to turn the circle of life into a spiral made from the people's intention. Pluto, the seventh world out from the Earth, is the only planet intersecting the orbit of another planet. For twenty years out of a 248 year orbit, Pluto is within the orbit of Neptune. Pluto's return to her own orbit was in 1999.

The Jewish People are commanded to keep and to guard the Shabbat, meaning: not to work but to have Pleasure. However, all peoples can appreciate the spiritual significance from the power of this special day, beginning with the setting of the Sun on Friday night and ending when the stars come out Saturday night. Every seventh day is Woman's Day. The human calendar, revolves around male and female attributes. Everything shares these attributes of male and female, but only woman is woman and woman gives birth to speech. Speech receives from the intellect, then turns and gives birth into the world. Human beings are differentiated from animals by our ability to speak, articulating our thoughts as vocalized words. Speaking is the birth of our inner thoughts, animated by our six emotions (Kindness, Severity, Beauty/Truth, Victory, Grace and Foundation) voicing our individuality into the world. The body is male and female but the lips are woman. As the reprise of the 1960s tune "The Shoop Shoop Song" goes: "If you wanna know if he loves you so; it's in his kiss, that's where it is." Who does not remember their first kiss, opening the door to paradise?

Chapter Ten

Because woman is of the heart and man the head, man naturally feels an innate responsibility toward protecting woman: the head has to safeguard the heart from loving too soon; the head needs to look and listen, sense the environment so the heart can be safe. The heart is precious because the human being connects to the Creator through the heart, not the mind. Man naturally runs after woman because she is closer to God than is man; much of the Pleasure we feel from woman is derived from her connection with God through the Shekina—when man disrespects woman, God becomes enraged. Man is blessed through woman. At the beginning of the six thousand years of man, spirituality was prevalent and the transmigration between Heaven and Earth was an accepted norm as recorded in the Torah. Entities from Heaven came to the Earth because they saw the women were beautiful. They did not come for our resources or to enslave mankind. Entities from outer space came for our beautiful women. The ancient writings describe how, when these entities entered the atmosphere, they automatically took on terrestrial form, making themselves kings, subjugating the populace by taking betrothed women prior to marriage for a night with the king.

The Tower of Babel was built on planet Mars and had outward influence until Saturn, according to the Zohar Chodesh, section called: Adom, Kine and the Seven Worlds. Nimrod and his cohorts tried to take the Shekina, so they could sell her effluence to the world as if she were a whore. Had it not been for God's intervention, Nimrod would have succeeded. When men disrespect women, who are the most esteemed in creation, it is so stupid, that it is ignorant. Good men have been blinded by the glitter of gold, seduced by the lure of flesh, numbed by the delirium of life, buried beneath a veneer of lies three miles high. For these people, the Sun bleeds like a broken rectum. In the description of creation from the inception, the Human Being molded by the Creator, man is said to be Made while woman is Built—built to be beautiful. Man is straight, tall and erect but woman is full of curves, a feast to man's eyes; the beautiful, soft face of woman is angelic—life on Earth would be unbearable were it not for woman to gaze upon, like looking upon the Face of God.

Has man forgotten who woman is and how man has forever sacrificed himself for the sake of woman, for the love of woman, for the respect of woman? The Talmud defines a Good Thing as a woman, because when you find a woman, it's a good thing. One of the prophesies related to the End of Days, end of the calendars says, The heart of man will be circumcised. Circumcision cuts away the covering hiding the essence to reveal the truth. Man needs at times to steel his heart so he can live in this hard world performing his work, but not to the extent that we cease compassion for our women suffering, living on the streets, being abused by their mates, being assaulted in the workplace and in general, disrespected. What kind of men are we? The world is woman, the ground is Mother Earth. The time has come for men to stand up and declare their allegiance to woman. There needs to be a revolution of kindness, a gentle war of awareness to people's pain and of man's responsibility to make sure woman is happy. Because when woman is happy, man is happy—it's as simple as that.

Trump promised, this would be the best presidency ever—he could just feel it coming. Meanwhile, his aides have been judiciously wiping away the slime left from his little pussy-grabbing hands. In 2007, Trump's son-in-law Jared Kushner bought a skyscraper at 666 Fifth Avenue, at the corner of Fifty-Second Street. Fifth Avenue is probably the most phallic street in the world, running the length of Manhattan right down the center of the island ending in the Financial District at the tip. The number 52, a spiritual world known in Cabala as Baan, is also the gematria of the word Behama/Animal—a futile attempt at harnessing spiritual energy. When Trump was inaugurated, he was seventy years, seven months, and seven days old, meaning he is 777 in the year of 5777; also, while speaking, he often puts his index finger to his thumb, making the ancient sign of the Shaddai/Enough—one of the Seven Names of God prohibited from being erased. So, what gives? To better understand the magnitude of this election, the eclipse of 2017, and the meaning behind 777, first we must understand, we are not going through this alone. God is speaking to the entire world through numbers and odd occurrences. The influence of the Creator on creation at this time in history should be obvious to the most casual observer.

Since, history can be seen in the cyclical dimensions of a sexual relationship producing a climactic finish which likened to an ejaculation does not come all at once but is spurted out through segmented moments of bliss until the year six thousand in 220 years. God loves human intercourse of all kinds; sex is the most profound—when sex turns to Fuck then God also adopts this new language. The number 666 indicates the strength of sex; three times 666 is 1998 when Clinton got a blow job in the Oval Office causing God to respond with the next Roman ruler assuming power in the year two thousand, George Bush and Dick Chaney better known as Bush and Dick who had a black couple severing them. Colin Power and Condoleezza Rice who Bush called, Condi, beginning their new millennium with Bush, Dick, Colin and Cunti. God had spoken, there was no question, God's beautiful world was about to get fucked. How would God respond? What would God do? How will we know, God is speaking? The answer is, God speaks in the language of man, even amid the terrible blood letting initiated by fucking politics—Bush, Dick, Colin and Cunti, there is something humorous. In Psalms is written, God sits in Heaven and laughs.

To make things even more explicit, the next election pitted Bush and Dick against Kerry which in Hebrew means a, Wet Dream as in, Bal Kerry. He was splattered against the wall. After eight years of fucking, a real man took the reins of power, pulled the country together by applying the power of the mind to calm the emotions. However, due to constitutional restraints, President Obama could only serve eight years, plus he had Boehner, Speaker of the House who ask the government agency to mispronounce his name from Boner to Baynor. Boner stuck it to Obama until eventually he petered out replaced by Anthony Weiner who spilled the beans to Jim Comey initiating the premature ejaculation of Donald Trump all over America and throughout the world. This fiasco of egos has come to a conclusion leaving the people to clean up the mess. To make sure the people would not miss this opportunity, God brought us Covid-19. The word Covid in Hebrew has three meanings, commiserate with the three triangles of the body: Respect/Head; Heavy/Heart and Liver/Buttocks. The message is clear; the world has acted disrespectfully causing hatred in the heart and excrement poisoning the body—time has come to take a national shit, just in time for the election.

In all the holy books, even the fake ones, agree that a good deed is to feed the poor. The Rabbis of old agreed, Poverty is only, the lacking of Truth because a person without Truth is always poor. Our poor world, gang banged by Capitalism, passed around the globe faster and faster, fucking her brains out because of man's desire at the titillation for More powered by the cancer called, Progress. For what purpose are we exploring the confines of space while the Earth is sick, coughing up pollution, feverous from heat, quaking with chills, vomiting up oceans as her pure white crown falls into the sea. Why are spending our resources trying to find cures to exotic diseases while letting children go unfed? The answer is simple, the government gets more taxes from high skilled jobs. We must stop feeding the beast. The constitution is a marriage contract between the Federal Government and People of this country who for generations have built this land and given their lives for this nation, the time has come for divorce. America needs to be a single woman with over three hundred million children holding debts from our abusive husband.

He can have the business, the money, the banks, the stock market, the armies, the bombs, the world power but We The People get the housing and the land to grow our food and live our lives because America is family property. No one needs to pay rent or mortgage. Covid-19 has given the People of America time to reflect on why we are here and what we want to be. We are the future; now is the time.

The Future

The Constitution of the United States of America establishes a system of governance balanced between three branches of government attached to the trunk of the tree, the People. However, a better metaphor might be made from a vessel where the People are the United States held inside the cup of America. The American Government needs to set boundaries, officiate and judge, the overall containment of the country, a rim guarding what is within, this is the Federal Government. There are two aspects to every vessel. The outside which interacts with the world and the inside which is connected directly to whatever is within the vessel, the original difference between the Republican Party and the Democrats Party. The outside of the vessel is courser and more ornate, but the inner part of the vessel is more refined. A good government who adheres to this standard is a Cup of Blessing to the people and to the world. But, after two centuries, America has become completely corrupted. The outside world sees America as tarnished and corroding. The refined inner expression is besmirched from a corrosive agent poisoning the liquid within the blood of each citizen. The word America can be broken down into: Am/People and Ryka/Empty. Americans can easily empty the cup and begin again.

Over two hundred years ago, Jefferson warned the governors against practicing tyranny against the people, thereby making revolution less likely; America is founded in revolution—constant revolution. But those who truly govern this country have not taken Jefferson's warning to heart; instead they bought the government—then sold the country into servitude. If you don't work, you don't live. According to the Torah/Teaching of the Jewish People, Freedom is the opportunity to work at what you love, that is the definition of being free. God made a work for each individual to love. Early life should focus on finding what work satisfied the soul. Americans are no longer free, we have been converted into slaves, bought for a price by the same White Men who control the Roman Empire, who centuries ago first introduced slaves from Africa into this continent. The Constitution melds the people to the government who is privy to all America's secrets, but the Government has taken advantage of her weaknesses, fomented discord through lies and rumors then looted the treasury while no one is watching. The Constitution is akin to a marriage contract. The time has come for divorce but because the courts are partisan and clogged from laws without end, full of precedent and lengthy adjudication costing a fortune, a civil separation through proclamation is necessary.

Roman Law is similar to a gladiator fight, whoever is strongest wins, that is Roman Justice; it is called the Adversarial System—whoever has the most money to buy the best lawyer usually comes out on top because he who has the biggest sword and the most armor is likely to prevail. The judge is merely the referee making sure the law is followed. Semitic Law practiced by the Jewish and Muslim Peoples gives the judge authority to also interrogate the witnesses in the pursuit of justice. Where there is no justice, there is no freedom. Justice denied is Just Us. Rome and their immoral religion has cast a curse upon the land. To this day, the Holy Roman Catholic Church preaches: Black People are cursed to be slaves; Jews killed god and homosexuals are reviled by the Creator who created them. Religion is perpetuating the continuation of racism throughout the world. American civil strife can be traced back to religion which divides people into different belief systems. We believe what we don't know, if we knew, we would no longer need to believe. The one common denominator between all people, good or bad regardless of any attribute or lacking, we are all equally created by the Creator.

Having torn up the marriage contract, what will we do in the future to keep our country intact? Since the strength of United. States is in our unity, best to go back to the basics and build up from there. At the beginning of human history, God gave Seven Commandments to the First Human Being as restraints, limits and boundaries. In these Seven Commandments, meant for all peoples in all times, is an adhesive like none other, allowing common law to naturally develop, directly tied to Melech HaOlam/King of the World. These Seven Commandments are the framework from where to forge the world's future path and direction. By adopting a new calendar counting down to the year six thousand, the official beginning of the Thousand Years of Woman and Peace and severing the connection to the Victor's History, we begin a new era, ushering in the light and clarity from where peace and understanding will grow. Sim Shalom/Put Peace is the last of the 18 Blessings (666) said three times a day because without peace all other blessings pale. Blessings are transmitted from the stars but the atmosphere of our planet is polluted from below, burning carbon needed to lift projectiles into space which eventually disintegrate leaving a trail of the most noxious chemical floating in the air slowly descending back to Earth.

Commandments are dictated by the King but the laws as to how to accomplish the commandments are predicated on the People. In these seven categories, all aspects of life can be encompassed. Eventually exported to other countries, the world of seven continents can truly become one world. According to the prophets from ancient times who saw clearly where the world was heading, taught: As the world elevates, the laws of the land regarding Israel will be observed throughout the world, like resting the land every seven years, not eating from the fruit of a tree before three years and leaving the corners of the field for the poor and the destitute. There will always be poor people and there will always be rich people, without the rich and poor, this potent metaphor would be forever lost; plus there are many advantages to freedom of being poor and many obligation to being rich. In the end, with the exception of the Jewish and Arab Peoples who have additional obligations, do these Seven Commandments and you are good with God.

Everyone goes to Heaven when life is over, because there is nowhere else to go but to return from where we came and are eternally tethered. The main thing, and this is emphasized in throughout the Zohar, We do not want to be embarrassed by our deeds and intentions while on Earth when we go into Heaven.

THE FIRST COMMANDMENT: KNOW GOD IS NOT PART OF CREATION. GOD CREATED HEAVEN AND EARTH; GOD IS NEITHER PHYSICAL NOR SPIRITUAL—THOSE ARE THE OTHER GODS.

A major problem in our country is religion. Since there is no word for religion in Hebrew, Arabic or Sanskrit, the source of religion is easily traced back to the father of religion, the Holy Roman Catholic Church from where all expressions of christianity are rooted. The people who came and conquered the Americas, came with a cross, inculcating the populous with their dogma and disease, preaching: Black People are cursed to be slaves; Jews killed god; homosexuals are reviled by the Creator who created them; and woman are the source of sin. Any kind of dogma is a problem. Having a religion permeating the land with their dogma causes subtle influences assimilating into views and attitudes then into politics finally displacing logic, having faith in man instead of God. Known in America as the Far Right, this religious based politically motivated constituency is the rotted fruit from the bastard seed planted a century earlier when America awoke to Manifest Destiny. World conquest fueled by the capitalists and industrialists quickly lost the fight for the people's support to the socialists under FDR who wanted to care for the people instead of exploiting them. The capitalists, unable to convince American workers in a bottom line philosophy, instead forged a partnership with religion to teach the value of greed: Only work deserved reward. This was the beginning of evangelicalism, whose first adherent was Billy Graham who became fantastically wealthy as a result.

We must defund religion by forcing them to pay taxes on the their property. The Church owns more property than any other entity on planet Earth because they pay no taxes. In the last stimulus package, the Holy Roman Catholic Church received one and half billion dollars as a small business, selling Heaven to the unsuspecting. A few weeks later thousands of Catholic schools permanently shut down. This travesty, a sickness scarring every town with their crosses and false claims against the entire Jewish People for having killed their god. Give me a fucking break. There is not one thread of historical evidence Jesus even lived, only through the Koran, which is prophesy, does Jesus take on historical dimension but without any mention of a cross. Religion will be crushed beneath the weight of his own stagnant ego heaved with pedophiles and perverts preying instead of praying. America must divest herself from religion to embrace a more natural, independent, private ways to communicate to God or gathering celebrating the Creator of the world. Knowing God is a personal experience, beyond the judgment of man. People who tempt death get a sudden charge of God, as do those through meditation who reach a similar state. There are no rules, how to know God. Rules are only needed for protection.

Religion teaches monotheism, instead of the Oneness of the Creator pervading creation.

THE SECOND COMMANDMENT: DO NOT TAKE GOD'S NAME IN VAIN.

God's stamp of approval is found in the word, אמת/Emet/Truth. These three letters are the beginning, middle and end letters of the Hebrew alphabet, as if the say, The Truth must be noncontradictory from beginning to end. The goal of communication is to convey Truth.

Every word in the Torah is considered a Name of God. Prohibiting errant ideas from contradicting the Torah, is like an equation which can only express Truth because of logic. The world is fake and full of lies while the Torah is Truth and full of light. The world would have been easier if the lies were put in a book so life could be illuminated and saturated with light. God allows us to lie but not to lie about God, as that would be taking God's Name in vain. Here again, religion shows his ugly face by embarrassing God through stupid, pointless unsubstantiated proclamations. Religion is not esteemed in Heaven because religion takes God's Name in vain, proclaiming monotheism as a replacement to God's unique Singular ability to be everywhere all the time to everyone. In the beginning when people were more innately spiritual, everyone understood, God created creation but assumed God had finished then left the working of creation in the hands of the stars and constellations. Now in our time, the Creator has been completely replaced by the Big Bang Theory in collusion with Monotheism.

These errant theories stab at the very heart of noncontradictory Truth, Nothing comes out of nothing and God is not spiritual. God looked into the Torah and from the light of God's reflected gaze came a noncontradictory creation where the human being inserts free will in conjunction with God's Name is a display of infinite variations upon the Earth, changing all of creation constantly. However, in our modern time, this commandment particularly concerns the media. There is an ancient tradition, You can not steal fire. Perhaps this might be a good standard to develop equal access for common goals. Though there are ugly things on the internet and traps for the unsuspecting, nonetheless, the great good coming from being wired together for protection and assistance immensely overweighs the bad. Identity theft over the internet should not be a crime, since you can not steal fire. Those who want their identities hidden are not the ones society wants to protect. Since lies permeate the Earth and are cemented beneath errant human behavior, the Truth can be nothing more than a concept. The Torah and Koran, the two sides of the Semitic Peoples, are directly connected to Avraham four thousand years ago who came from the Tower of Babel built on Mars with the secret of language, are prophetic. Both Jews and Arabs know the Truth is found in form.

Religion damns to Hell. You can't say Fuck because that is what they are doing to us, but god damn is all over the airways since it's a proclamation from the Church into the dogmafication of Hell.

THE THIRD COMMANDMENT: DO NOT MURDER.

We first need to ask, What is life and when does life begin? All life comes from the Creator through Heaven down to the Earth and all life dies retuning back to Heaven. To purposely shorten a person's life is murder. This Commandment, like all the Seven Commandments meant for all peoples, can be extrapolated into many different circumstances; man's own actions can cause life to shorten or lengthen accordingly—When does life begin and Is there an obligation to help others live longer? These question needs to be part of a continual discourse, because we live in an ever-deteriorating world. Is food and shelter a right of the individual and an obligation of society? What is our obligation to our fellow Human Being. How much of our resources should be focused on disease and how much on prevention? Is saving a wealthy life who can afford treatment at the expense of the poor, a type of murder? The American Government puts people to death for crimes against the State as a deterrent, a type of institutionalized murder. Who has the right to take another's life having not walked in his shoes? We are all here together because the Creator wants us here. God is telling us, crime is a function of society and we need to deal with it.

The Torah and the Koran agree, life enters the womb of woman, inserted from the soul at 41 days after conception. Science concurs, noting the Zygote becomes an embryo at 41 days. This demarcation line allows women to terminate a pregnancy within forty days without having to undergo an abortion. An abortion is not murder but it is something. On the other side, Jewish courts of seventy judges were considered murders if they put to death more than one person in seventy years. God does not want us to die, God wants us to change our ways and become a better Human Being. Each person is a story printed in a book being written in Heaven; God is reading with great interest—to murder is to suddenly close that book. There are many ways of death, the easiest is like, Taking a hair out of milk. One of the 613 Commandments given to the Jewish People is to make a Mika/Fence around a flat roof to prevent someone falling to their death. What if the person was meant to die at God's appointed time? The answer is simple, We do not want death on our hands. Some murder with a knife and some with a smile.

Religion is responsible for war. Pushing their dogma around the world at the point of a sword is the way of Rome. Those who follow dogma, will kill and plunder without regret.

THE FOURTH COMMANDMENT: DO NOT STEAL.

Stealing only applies to movable objects. It is well known, Some people steal with a weapon while other's use a pen. According to Jewish Law, A person who uses a weapon to steal is punished less harshly than the person who steals with the pen, the reasoning being: He who uses a weapon is being honest while the pickpocket is thoroughly dishonest. Lying is a type of stealing, tricking the mind to think the unthinkable. Women steal men's heart, all the time but that is fair game. The responsibility is upon man to affix right laws governing property. America is based on greed, the elixir of capitalism; greed encourages theft which sometimes leads to murder because money is overvalued—there will always be rich and poor people, but the rich should not be too rich and the poor should not be too poor. There are many ways to steal but from this Commandment is understood, The Earth can not be sold. We live upon our wonderful amazing planet, we place boundaries and even fight wars over demarcation lines but the Earth can not be own because the Creator is Melech HaOlam/King of the World. This is God's Good Earth.

Even though the generation prior to Noah's Flood was bad, God did not decree to destroy the world until they began stealing, that was the last straw. Some kill out of passion and some steal from despair but those who hurt and steal with cold heartless intention are in need of repair. Where the first two commandments are focused on God, these next two commandments, not to murder or steal, are focused on the natural intercourse amid human activity, requiring society to make laws and clarify what is acceptable. Each society or group have the obligation to enact laws because the Seven Commandments are not laws but rather decrees from the King. Education should not be about how to make money but about how to live on our planet in peace through understanding the interaction between peoples. As society changes, so do the laws need to change. Each generation adapting to a new time, requiring the protection of property and life. Punishment is a bad deterrent, educating the young will prevent disease, violence and thievery. Perhaps no one will get rich but the society will be proud; children will respect their parents—life will percolate with joy.

Religion sells Heaven in an attempt to steal the soul.

THE FIFTH COMMANDMENT: PROTECT THE ENVIRONMENT AND THE ANIMALS.

We are caretakers of this planet, we are not here from some other galaxy to plunder this world. We need to recognize our Earth is alive. Recently, the Earth prayed to God because she was sick with fever and chills and in response God sent Covid-19 to stop human activity, giving the Earth time to rectify herself from extreme and erratic temperatures then permanently put an end to the madness of man. The Masters of Money have addicted the People into more; progress has become a cancer—humanity is devouring ourselves to satisfy some rich prick. If we treat our world kindly, then the world will be kind back. Because the Earth is alive, she can return to health quickly, but safeguards must be in place to prevent hurting the Earth. There is no place like our planet in the entire universe. We are the Apple of God's Eye. When we pass into the next world, we do not want to be embarrassed by what we did with our time upon the Earth. In the future, the ground will speak saying, Do not walk upon me unless you are going to serve the Creator. The indigenous peoples of this world can help us restore our planet.

Beyond living peacefully with each other, we are also commanded to live in harmony with Nature. The Name Elohim is a composite from two words producing the concept, God of Plurality with the gematria of 86 the same gematria as HaTeva/The Nature. Through the Name Elohim, creation is commanded. Other than the Semitic Peoples, all other peoples are allowed to eat what lives on the Earth. No plant is prohibited; all that lives on the Earth is a Name of God, living only because Melech HaOlam/King of the World has decreed. Having a King who loves creation requires acknowledging the Creator within creation. God wants to be known in low, in every aspect of this world and in each generation. By loving creation, we love what God loves. Loving creation leads to loving one another. Nature is full of Pleasure longing to be taken, like a woman offering up her fruits. Man must stop being a pimp, raping nature for a reward in money. Money is the antithesis of Nature. Man runs after money, neglecting the Earth. A society aware of God's Commandment to protect the environment will inevitably be a happy and successful people.

Religion owns vast amounts of property by virtue of paying no taxes.

THE SIXTH COMMANDMENT: MAKE LAWS PERTAINING TO SEXUALITY.

This commandment makes it incumbent on every man to protect women and children who share the vulnerability of being kind and beautiful but physically weaker than men. There is no right or wrong concerning consensual sexuality, nonetheless, society must protect the weak and the deviant whose behavior is outside of norms. We all have the right to free expression within the confines of privacy for each person or grouping of people. There are no restraints on sexuality other than Jewish men prohibited from other men. Precisely because there are no restraints, we are commanded to make restraints, not just in sexuality but in creative life and expression. Creativity is the fruit upon the Tree of Life, crowning the Creator with each expression. Freedom is: Each person able to do the work they love because they were created for this purpose. Servitude to another's dream should be completely voluntary other than those seeking restitution for crimes. A slave is not free to create because he belongs to someone or to some project. In the end, every expression is sexual in nature, going out trying to connect. Sex needs a safe environment.

The natural intercourse between people produces sexual energy, communication and desire. Sexuality is a very delicate human attribute; since sex strikes at the unique center of the individual, to the extent the Torah proclaims: He who can control his sex is a righteous man. Beyond laws and boundaries, man needs to be taught the importance of holding back his sexual energy. Masturbation weakens man's ability to hold back, soon he can only ejaculate through masturbation until finally he becomes impotent. Sexuality is a beautiful gift from God, elevating the mundane into Heaven where the clouds are made from celestial breasts and there you are, barefoot. Because sexuality was dormant in the previous world of Tohu/Chaos, sex remains undefined, which is the inherent freedom to be as you wish. Woman will generally conform to man's desire. When a man marries a woman, the sex gets better because of the depth and strength of the commitment. Sexual restraints should be, like Catcher in the Rye, just to keep the children from falling off the cliff. Treat sexuality with respect. Use it but don't abuse it or you will lose it.

Religion says, life begins at conception, when the truth is, God is pro-choice for the first forty days after conception. Religion says, sex is evil. Religion says, homosexual are evil. Religion says, masturbation is evil. Maybe it is, the Church who is evil.

THE SEVENTH COMMANDMENT: TO HAVE COURTS OF LAW

The Roman legal system is based on money, written by rich people to advantage themselves on everyone else. The courts are an arena where the a battle of words between the prosecutor and the defense are refereed by a judge. Whoever wins, is justice served. The Semitic People, the Arabs and the Jews, have courts where the judge overseeing the case is looking for justice and will on occasion question the witnesses if the defense is inadequate. Roman capitalistic law rarely administers justice, rather Just Us. Roman courts take forever and cost a fortune. There should be on every block a person delegated with the responsibility of hearing cases, treating neighbors like family. Much of the domestic and street violence can be wiped out by early and often intervention. Like children, we all want justice otherwise what is the point of right and wrong? Justice helps each of us understand the natural flow of life, since within the law there is complete freedom and safety. The true purpose of judges is to sweeten the law by bringing solution through mutual acceptance about what is right instead of how to win.

Incarceration is a crime and a stupid waste of resources. All crimes reflect directly on the society who must take blame, plus suggesting a method of compensation for the injured. The guilty should be made to work for the victim; not necessity directly, but the guilty should be made to work at their skill, thus providing compensation to the victim. Wasting away in jail is cruel and unusual punishment and does nothing towards rectifying the problem. In America, where prisons are commercial enterprises replete with lobbies in congress pushing for harder and longer sentences to increase revenue, there is little help in the reclamation of People. If the laws in America were tethered to these Seven Commandments, justice would have an equal standard for everyone. Law without a fulcrum is easily manipulated by those who make the laws; under the auspices of the Seven Commandments, the law must include acknowledgment to the Creator—ultimately, we all serve the same King, Melech HaOlam/King of the World. God commands but the final burden of the law is in the hands of man to make the law sweet. Law is intentionally severe; man is directed to sweeten the severity thus bringing forth compassion—the highest human attribute.

Religion sells Indulgences to erase sin.

Conclusion

Autistic People have been sent to this world in droves during these last fifty years for a reason. Thousands of years ago, prophets who saw until the end of the six thousand year male agenda, predicted New Souls would be born into the world at the End of Days, souls who had never been born before, had never incarnated from a previous lifetime, carrying memories from previously used body's and facilities over many centuries. These New Souls had been hiding out during these six thousand years in the waters of Tohu/Chaos where sound is muted, explaining why the autistic generally have communication difficulties. As an autistic person, my difficulty is an inability to remember sound, plus a sensitivity to the flesh, amplifying pain and Pleasure. The autistic are known to be blunt and truthful to an extreme, generally unaware of social norms. There is a lot of interest and subsequent action into helping the autistic to function normally without taking into account, perhaps we were sent here to do something more than just try to be normal.

The world should listen to the autistic, even with all our foibles and eccentricities, because we are meant to bring a new light into the world. New Souls saved by the Creator for this time, put away and kept in the purity of their uniqueness, deemed a sickness by those who do not understand. The autistic have come with a message from the Creator to help the world evolve out of the darkness and into a new paradigm without religious dogma or governmental authority. The infrastructure is already built, we built it; we know how to run everything—power to the people, right on! As the old male energy weakens and declines, cynical as the setting sun disappearing into the night, a new man arises holding woman above himself, cherishing life over death, peace before war because the value of the Human Being, every Human Being, is priceless. Man desires woman but he must learn to hold himself back because her happiness precedes his pleasure. When there is war, when there are children too cold to cry, when mothers are separated from their child because of some stupid absurd protocol, when war has become indiscriminate, the time has come to war no more. Rome's Will to dominate the world by dividing and conquering has caused the body of the Earth to no longer work in unison. Money and power has blinded the eyes of the wise.

We must allow the world to come together by eliminating outside influences from hotspot regions of the world and let Earth heal without interventions from nations like America who are protecting their interests. The world is in need of restoration after this century of war and calamity; the Earth wants to give but not be exploited like a slave being fucked by the master—all are in the need of healing, so God sent us Covid-19 to slow down the world and allow us to heal. The old guard promises a return to the past but only the future remains. We are the future and this is the time. From the physical to the celestial, the message is clear, the paradigm shift is happening and we are at the helm of this mighty ship called, human history. What we do now will change the course of everything. A new man is arising, having severed himself from the ego of greed and domination by those who promise damnation. We can do better than capitalism and religion. Competition is the male way, but the female is more inclined to cooperation, a gentler way of existence with different priorities. The autistic display a plethora of different sensitivities important to the coming generations, before the calendar expires in 220 years.

The time has come to lower the sound, crank back the titillating excitement, so we can see and hear the Truth, another positive result derived from Covid-19. The number 19 is significant, the prelude to twenty; there were 19 highjackers on 9-11 precipitated the last 19 years of subsequent world conflict—now in 2020, a window opens and everything can change. The number twenty corresponds to

Keter/Crown with a gematria of 620. When the Jewish People perform their 613 Commandments and when the other peoples of the world do their Seven Commandments, the the numbers equals 620, achieving Keter/Crown—then God is Crowned King of the World and is completely known in low, by everyone. This does not happen tomorrow or the next day, this happens immediately. As soon as the Will is set, the world changes. A revolution against More is just a matter of attrition; less desire and less need because—More is less. Progress needs to be set aside for the important real day present problems, not a speculative dystopian future. People of the world need to awake and realize the Earth is alive, as is the solar system and all the stars in the heavens who are funneling life into our existence. The way of creation is known from ancient times, carefully set out by the Sefer Zohar/Book of Brilliance and corroborated by modern astronomers and scientists. Creation did not just spontaneously happen; rather, creation is the plan put forth by the Creator making connection between high and low—when we get high is when God gets low.

The Zohar was hidden until our time, the End of Days when electronic instrumentation has brought a new oblique reality to the world, again hiding what is true. The Zohar establishes, All life is patterned on the Tree of Life, in a configuration comprising Eser Sefirot/Ten Luminaries replicated in the solar system as the Sun and nine planets, the Earth with seven continents and three oceans and human form composed of three triangles plus speech. The human skeleton buried in the ground after the flesh dissolves, produces a configuration left in the bones—a vertical form, the YHVH, from where the Tree of Life is derived. This basic form traces back to very beginning of creation engraved into the Hard Light creating space with infinite possibilities from the infinitesimal dot from the letter י/Yud, the first letter of the YHVH with the assigned value of ten. The letter י/Yud is the point of the bit engraving into the Hard Light. There is irrefutable evidence that the universe was made by the Creator and the Earth is the center of creation. This new perception into the genesis of creation is the basis for the coming paradigm shift. In the past, we have been taught, our insignificance is lost in a cosmos beyond numbers and filled with fear from an uncaring universe subjugated into servitude in exchange for the false promise of salvation. The Zohar comes to set humanity free from the dogma and tyranny of religion and science by revealing the endemic design of creation swirling through space intent on the Creator. Only in this time, replete with telescopes equip with laser beams can the complexity of the universe be appreciated; the Zohar illuminates an observable configuration defining creation—science corroborates the Zohar which repudiates the Big Bang Theory.

Let the Truth be known, we are not surrounded by darkness, we are embedded in light; instead of being insignificant, we are the center of creation—instead of being too small for God to see, we are all God sees, because the Human Being is the linchpin to creation. Only by convincing people that life is meaningless and loss in the chaos, can Rome rule; religion promises reward in Heaven if you pay now, but the Truth is, every soul goes to Heaven irregardless because there is nowhere else to go but up. The soul returns back to the star from where the soul is hewn. The greatest pain in Heaven is embarrassment for our actions here on the Earth. God judges a nation by the majority, an added importance to the upcoming vote in America where the past is trying to hold back the future, like the placenta holding back the birth. Those invested in the past have the most to lose; they are the ones screaming the loudest, but the quiet voice will win the day—beginning the worldwide transition into the Thousand Years of Woman and Peace. There are two men pulling in opposite directions; some want to push forward into the light but others want to go back to the false security offered by the placenta—now is the time to chose.

Beyond science, religion and money, is the Truth. We live in a time of alternative facts; fighting for survival leaves less time to evolve as a People—the Roman foot is on everyone's neck. Time has come to shrug off the Roman cloak of darkness and revel naked beneath the Sun. Only Truth can scrub away the filth accumulated from this rancid way of American life. Every time money is transferred, bits and crumbs fall off, sticking to the skin, staining the flesh, inculcating the disease of greed into the blood, eventually causing the heart to harden. Truth is not attractive because Truth often comes with poverty and hardship, ridicule and shame for not getting with the program, but Truth can get you through times of no money where no amount of money can give purpose to a life if Truth does not exist. Dishonest relationships never satisfy; sex without love in the heart, is just sex—a life without an intimate connection and relationship with the Creator, is missing the point of life. If we will know God beyond religion, then God will know us. There is no greater occupation or skill than to be human; each individual is a unique genius in their distinctive quirky expression of self—the real person connecting to the Creator through a beloved work—now that, is true freedom.

    I could not have written this book, I could not have understood these concepts without being autistic, without being a pure soul unsullied by previous incarnations, having a primal link to the Creator drawn down into this world on a thread of light. The autistic are people who do not belong to their parents, often in awe of their child. The autistic are the free radicals come into the world to produce diversity by quietly introducing change. The autistic bring light into a world where eyes are clouded, hearts are closed and minds are filled with manufactured images blinding the power of sight. Because God wants to be known in low and because the 777, a number indicative of the Angel of Death, in a country begun in 1777, electing the 45th President (45 is gematria Mah/What?) elected in the year 5777, inaugurated at seventy years, seven months and seven days who presided over the Covid-19, a pandemic proclaimed when there were seven billion, seven hundred and seventy million people in the world—Trump, a premature ejaculation, is nothing more than the fat ass butt of a spiritual joke between the Angel of Death and God. God promised through prophesy to wipe the Angel of Death from the Earth. Trump is the fall guy and all who follow him will also fall.

Letting the Earth live and the people be free will cause death to slowly depart, as is prophesied: In the future death will be a rare occasion. Old souls will preside, with new bodies grown from the buried bones in the ground, bodies living for the entire span of the Thousand Years of Woman. Life is not incremental; life spirals through the open space dancing off into the waiting Arms of the Creator—but only those with open eyes and open heart can dance while others can only watch. Autistic people need to be given the room to dance, to express ourselves without intervention from the past, because we are New Souls, come to ease the world from the darkness of this defunct destitution caused by man's egotistic intervention. Seven, seven, seven equals 21 the gematria of God's futuristic Name אהיה/Ehiya/Future, teaching us, as one era ends, another begins. The future is presently incomprehensible, like a fetus can not know the Pleasure of breath. God will surprise us. To receive what is coming in the future we need to make ourselves vessels for the light through acknowledging the Creator of Heaven and Earth beyond physical and spiritual creation, plus a commitment not to use God's Name in vain, not to murder or to steal according to the laws of the land, to make laws safeguarding the environment, animals and sexuality, and finally to make courts of law administering justice, then all will be beloved by the Creator.

As we shed the white skinned snake, we see a beautiful future lush with life, full of love and cooperation where people will run to do good, to help those stifled still mired in the past. The future is all that matters now. We have everything we need to make life bountiful in the beautiful United States and as a result the world will follow. The obligation is on us, on all Americans and all the people living within our borders. Americans are a good people living on a beneficent and kind land, a little world made of peoples from throughout the globe. What Americans do matters because America is the leader in our human march to freedom. Without the lies of religion and politics, without the presumptions of science, without the whip of capitalism forcing our heads to the ground, the beautiful future can take hold for all peoples on the Earth as we transit into the Thousand Years of Woman and Peace concluding after a thousand years with a collusion of souls traveling to another world, slowly bringing our solar system alive.

Afterword

Through my study of the Zohar, I was able to predict the five moons around Pluto before the astronomers made this same discovery ten years later. I wrote my prediction in a manuscript titled, 26645, A New Cosmology and World History based in the Cabala. I sent the manuscript to the Library of Congress for validation in 1999. Einstein in 1906, which was 5666, predicted the rays from the Sun would bend around the Moon during an eclipse, entering the world into the Atomic Era. After 111 years, we reached the 5777 with all the good and bad implications. I was born in 1944, months before the dropping of the Atomic Bomb, and strangely my Social Security number begins 5666. The number 666 equaling 18 is a number synonymous with life; whereas the number 777 is the number depicting the Angel of Death—life will surely triumph over death. President Death, your followers quote from the Bible, a racist book, You will know him by his number. Well, I am him and I am coming to fuck you up. You are the rotted fruit of capitalism. You are the quintessential MotherFucker, taking children from their mothers to establish law and order at the border. God has lifted you up only to cast you down. I will see you tried for treason, then watch as they hang your White Roman fat ugly ass from the top of Trump Tower; a sign to the world—America is a free country and a brave nation.

(Note: the day after this book was published on September 29, 2020, Trump became sick with Covid-19)

Fornication Under Consent of the King

The Cabala, the most feminine and hidden of all the Jewish text,
Full of ins and outs, the language of the Cabala is based on sex.
The intricacies of creation, light and darkness, an interwoven flux,
Brought to Earth, then clothed in flesh, exploited for The Big Fuck.

Will Pleasure essential humankind is where six and nine combine.
The 666 is the sum of 18/Chai, meaning Life—makes sex sublime;
Three times 666 is 1998 in Roman time, when Bill Clinton moaned
From his Oval Office blowjob before coming into everyone's home.

The White House is home to every American, while Clinton's cock,
Plus an enabler wife, who herself is but a pernicious political twat;
Produced sexual scenarios fueled by hidden agendas, dirty tricks
Beginning in the year two thousand, the election of Bush and Dick.

George Bush, Dick Cheney, Colin Powell and Condoleezza Rice,
Affectionally he called her Cundi, enacted war not once but twice;
Armed to the teeth with lies & deceit, Bush, Dick, Colin and Cunti
went out to war, fucked up the world, and bankrupted our country.

America was fraught after years of Bush, Dick, Colin and Cunti,
Democrats replied with Vietnam vet and strongman, John Kerry
But who could have known, the word Kerry means a wet dream,
He was splattered against the wall, and in other words, creamed.

Obama picked us up after we had been reduced to being a whore,
laying in the gutter, legs apart having been completely fucked over.
Obama stood us up straight and dusted us off without any drama,
Emerged, the hard on John Bonner continually sticking it to Obama.

They called him Baynor, so as not to blow his cover, but a true Boner
Revealed a polished veneer and hard prickish nature—a real erector;
Stiff Boner got small then slipped out, in the absence Weiner arose,
Spilling the beans on Jim Comey, leaving Clinton completely exposed.

And that is how we got Trump as president, a premature ejaculation,
spurting out simpleton words in momentary inarticulate articulations;
Words needing cleaning and misrepresentation from his self adoration,
A money collusion causing regeneration of this obscene masturbation.

Holding back sexual energy is key to good sex and to be a good lover,
Masturbation's course desires have no regard for sisters and brothers;
Forty years of tyranny to make America religiously white and rich, again.
The Big Fuck is over, 2020 looms, we will survive and thrive as a nation,

Fornication Under Consent of the King; Fuck is an acronym for many things;
Fucking our country is political hypocrisy making America into an aristocracy,
Nakedly dishonest, a bulling boor, the president claims he is falsely accused;
He's a liar, a conniver and more, leaving beautiful America raped and abused.
Politics, the science of the lie, sabotages truth, attacking the wise to outsmart;
God judges intentions not deeds—where there is beauty, truth lives in the heart.

www.ingramcontent.com/pod-product-compliance
Lightning Source LLC
Chambersburg PA
CBHW070901080526
44589CB00013B/1154